Titles previously published in
YOUR PERSONAL HEALTH SERIES

Alzheimer's Disease

Arthritis

The Complete Breast Book

Crohn's Disease and Ulcerative Colitis

Depression and Bipolar Disorders

Eating Disorders

Epilepsy and Seizures

Eyes

Hepatitis C

Migraine

Multiple Sclerosis

The Pain Relief Handbook

Sleep

Stroke

When a Child Has Diabetes

CANADIAN MEDICAL ASSOCIATION

This book is endorsed by the Canadian Medical Association. The association's mission is to serve and unite the physicians of Canada and be the national advocate, in partnership with the people of Canada, for the highest standards of health and health care.

Canadian Medical Association Advisor

John Howard, MD, FRCPC
Professor of Medicine and Paediatrics
University of Western Ontario
London, ON

YOUR PERSONAL HEALTH SERIES

ASSOCIATION MÉDICALE CANADIENNE · CANADIAN MEDICAL ASSOCIATION

Crohn's Disease & Ulcerative Colitis

Fred Saibil, MD

KEY PORTER BOOKS

National Library of Canada Cataloguing in Publication

Saibil, Fredric G., 1942–
  Crohn's disease & ulcerative colitis / Fred Saibil.—2nd rev. ed.

(Your personal health series)
Includes index.
"Canadian Medical Association".
ISBN-10: 1-55263-543-0, ISBN-13: 978-1-55263-543-8

1. Enteritis, Regional—Popular works. 2. Ulcerative colitis—Popular works.
I. Canadian Medical Association. II. Title. III. Title: Crohn's disease and ulcerative colitis. IV. Series.

RC862.I53S25   2003   616.3'44   C2003-902794-5

The publisher gratefully acknowledges the support of the Canada Council for the Arts and the Ontario Arts Council for its publishing program.

We acknowledge the financial support of the Government of Canada through the Book Publishing Industry Development Program (BPIDP) for our publishing activities.

Key Porter Books Limited
Six Adelaide Steet East, Tenth floor
Toronto, Ontario
Canada M5C 1H6

www.keyporter.com

Design: Peter Maher
Diagrams: Martyn Lengden
Electronic formatting: Heidy Lawrance Associates

Printed and bound in Canada

07 08 09 10 9 8 7 6

Contents

Introduction / vii

Chapter One: The Normal GI System and IBD / 1

Chapter Two: Who Gets IBD? What Causes It? / 9

Chapter Three: Symptoms and Signs / 19

Chapter Four: How Is IBD Diagnosed? / 28

Chapter Five: Diet and IBD / 35

Chapter Six: Drugs and IBD / 57

Chapter Seven: Surgery for IBD / 105

Chapter Eight: Children with IBD / 142

Chapter Nine: Complications of IBD / 146

Chapter Ten: Cancer and IBD / 166

Chapter Eleven: Living with IBD / 171

Chapter Twelve: Looking Ahead / 193

Table of Drug Names / 195

Glossary / 197

Further Resources / 207

Index / 209

Introduction

The term "inflammatory bowel disease" (IBD) refers to Crohn's disease and ulcerative colitis, two closely related conditions that cause persistent or recurring inflammation of one or more parts of the intestine. Whereas Crohn's disease can affect any part of the gastrointestinal system, from the mouth to the anus, ulcerative colitis occurs only in the colon (large intestine, large bowel).

A Scottish surgeon named Dalziel was one of the first people to describe what we now call Crohn's disease. In 1913 he published a paper about nine patients who had intestinal inflammation with certain typical features. However, Crohn's disease is named after the late Dr. Burrill Crohn. He and his colleagues at the Mount Sinai Medical Center in New York City re-emphasized Dalziel's findings in a series of papers in 1932.

Although these diseases are common, it is only in the past twenty to twenty-five years that it has become acceptable to talk about them publicly. Heart disease, diabetes, and even cancer have been freely discussed for many years, but no one wanted to hear about diarrhea, bloody bowel movements, or the need for frequent, urgent trips to the bathroom. The causes of these conditions are unknown. For years they were thought to be due to stress, but this is not the case. There is no known cure for Crohn's disease; ulcerative colitis can be cured, but only by surgical removal of the whole colon, including the rectum.

IBD can start at any age, but usually begins in the late teens or early adulthood or – less often – in middle age. Both Crohn's disease and ulcerative colitis are sometimes associated with a variety of medical problems outside of the intestine, including arthritis, skin conditions, kidney stones, cancer, and gallstones, among others.

Managing a chronic disease requires a team effort, and the team consists of the patient (and possibly the patient's family), the doctor (and possibly additional doctors), and sometimes other healthcare professionals. If patients are taught which problems they can treat (or at least start to treat) themselves, and which ones should be promptly reported, they achieve a greater degree of independence. For many patients, this means being able to go about their daily lives without worry.

This book, which is aimed primarily at patients and their families, provides a comprehensive review of IBD. Every effort has been made to avoid complex medical terminology. When such terms are necessary, definitions are provided in the text or in the glossary.

Topics covered include the signs, symptoms, and complications of IBD; nutritional issues, including lactose intolerance and other causes of gas and diarrhea; standard and newer treatments; surgery, with explanations of both minor and major operations; problems relating particularly to children with IBD; and various issues affecting everyday life, as well as self-help strategies for dealing with them.

Remember, this book is designed to educate you, not to frighten you. Having IBD can be difficult, but you can learn to live with it – and to fight back. This book will help you do that.

O N E

The Normal GI System and IBD

The Normal Gastrointestinal System

Learning about a medical subject is much like learning about anything else. You have to start with the basics and build on that. To learn about diseased bowel, you first have to learn about healthy bowel.

The bowel is part of the gastrointestinal system, commonly referred to as the gastrointestinal tract, or GI tract, for short. The GI tract begins at the mouth and ends with the anal canal. Most of it lies in the abdominal cavity, which is lined with a thin, transparent tissue called the *peritoneum*. The chief function of the GI tract is to digest food – break it down into usable materials, then absorb them and eliminate the waste products.

When you eat, food goes from your *mouth* down your *esophagus* (the swallowing tube), into your *stomach*. Your stomach grinds the food and dilutes it. The resulting semiliquid gradually empties into the *small bowel*, or small intestine, which is 10 to 20 feet (3 to 6 meters) long and lies coiled in the middle of your abdomen.

The small bowel is made up of three parts. The first is the *duodenum*, which is just a few inches (centimeters) long. The next part, about 5 to 10 feet (1.5 to 3 meters) long, is

The Gastrointestinal Tract

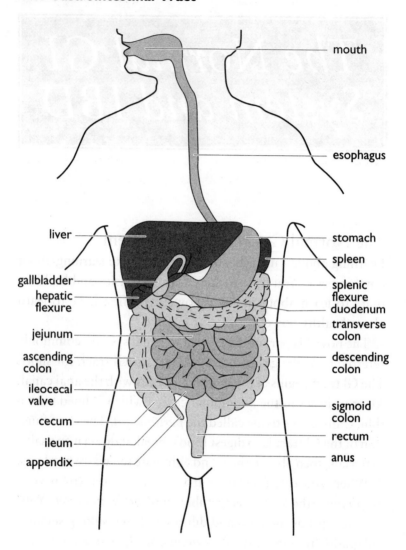

the *jejunum*. This is where most of the food that we eat is digested and absorbed. The last 5 to 10 feet of the small bowel is the *ileum*. The juices produced by all three parts of the small intestine, as well as juices from the liver, gallbladder, and pancreas, digest (break down) food and convert it into usable elements. Most carbohydrates (e.g., breads, potatoes, and pasta) and proteins (e.g., meat, eggs, fish) are broken down and absorbed in the jejunum. Fats (e.g., butter, oil, margarine) are digested more slowly and require both the jejunum and ileum to be absorbed. Two things are absorbed exclusively by the ileum: vitamin B_{12} and bile salts. This point becomes important when people undergo surgery to remove this part of the small bowel.

The ileum runs into the *colon*, low down on the right side of the abdomen. At the junction of the ileum and colon is a muscular thickening known as the *ileocecal valve*. It is not really a valve, but it opens and closes like a valve. This permits the small bowel to discharge its contents (mainly waste products) intermittently into the colon.

The colon, also known as the large bowel or large intestine, is much wider than the small intestine and is about 5 feet (1.5 meters) long. It too has different sections. The first is the *cecum*, which is a little cul-de-sac that lies below the junction of the ileum and the colon. The cecum probably does not have any specific function but is a remnant of evolution. The same may be true for the *appendix*, which projects from the cecum, although the appendix contains a lot of lymphoid tissue (part of the immune system) and this may be important.

Running upward from the cecum is the *ascending colon*. As you follow it, you will come to a sharp bend called the *hepatic flexure*. "Flexure" means "bend"; "hepatic" (from the Greek word "hepar," "liver") indicates that the bend is at the liver.

The segment of colon that runs from the hepatic flexure across the abdomen is called the *transverse colon*. The colon then turns sharply again at the *splenic flexure* (at the spleen).

The segment of colon that runs downward from the splenic flexure is called the *descending colon*. Following the descending colon is the *sigmoid colon*, named after the Greek letter *sigma* ("s") because the sigmoid curves frequently.

The *rectum* makes up the last section of the colon, although it is often treated as a separate entity. The *anal canal* is the outlet for the rectum. It is surrounded by the *anal sphincter*, a valvelike muscle that controls the passage of stool (waste matter) out of the rectum. The *anus* is the opening at the end of the canal.

These different sections of the colon do not have distinctive functions. The terms for the various sections of the colon allow doctors to communicate more precisely with other doctors when describing a problem.

The colon has two main functions. One is to store waste material. The other is to absorb salt and water.

The terms "stool" and "feces" (pronounced fee-sees) refer to the material discharged from the rectum, whether it is solid or liquid. When the stool starts out near the cecum, it is brown water – it looks just like a polluted river! When the stool comes out of the rectum, it is supposed to be a nice, neat package – not too hard, not too soft, not too big, not too small – about 12 inches long and sausage-shaped. As the brown fluid moves around the colon, the water is gradually absorbed by the lining of the colon so that the stool becomes more and more solid.

About 75 percent of a normal stool in the rectum is water. The GI tract is full of millions of different germs, mainly bacteria, mostly in the colon. They have a short life span and are constantly dying and being replaced by newly born bacteria; live and dead bacteria contribute about 8 percent to the bulk of the stool. About 4 percent comes from undigested food roughage (fiber). The lining of the whole GI tract replaces itself approximately every 72 hours, which means that a layer of dead tissue regularly "peels off"; this makes up about 3 percent of stool. The colon is always producing mucus, which is nature's lubricant, and this also ends up in the stool (1 percent). The remaining 9 percent is composed of a variety of substances.

When your rectum fills with stool, a message is sent to your brain telling it that the rectum needs to be emptied. If you sit on the toilet, the rectum will contract (squeeze), the anal sphincter will open, and the stool will be pushed out through the anal canal into the toilet. The normal process of digestion will have been completed.

Inflammatory Bowel Disease (IBD)

Inflammation – the word means "being set on fire" – is a localized protective response that occurs when tissue is damaged or destroyed. Its purpose is to wall off, dilute, or destroy an injurious agent. Acute inflammation is characterized by pain, heat, redness, and swelling. Chronic inflammation is a less dramatic process. It may proceed without any of these features, yet it results in distortion, and sometimes destruction, of tissues, often leading to permanent scarring.

Inflammatory bowel disease is just that – disease in which the bowel becomes inflamed. By convention the term refers to just two diseases: ulcerative colitis (UC) and Crohn's disease (CD).

Both UC and CD probably first appeared as isolated cases several centuries ago, but they did not attract medical interest until the last half of the nineteenth century. Ulcerative colitis was described and named in 1875 in a medical textbook published in London, England. In 1913, Dalziel's article in a British journal mentioned a group of patients with what was probably Crohn's disease. But it wasn't until a more widely publicized report was published in the United States in 1932 by Dr. Crohn and his colleagues that the disease came to be known as Crohn's disease.

It is common for different doctors to make up new names for specific diseases, especially those of unknown cause. Sometimes multiple names occur because what were thought to be two separate diseases turn out to be one and the same. For example, Crohn's disease was originally thought to occur only in the small intestine, and not in the colon.

Other Names for Ulcerative Colitis and Crohn's Disease

Ulcerative colitis (UC)
- idiopathic ulcerative colitis (idiopathic means "of unknown cause")
- idiopathic proctocolitis
- nonspecific ulcerative colitis

Crohn's disease (CD)
- ileitis, terminal ileitis ("terminal" refers to the terminus or end of the ileum)
- regional enteritis, regional ileitis
- granulomatous ileitis/enteritis/colitis ("granulomatous" refers to a specific appearance under the microscope)
- Crohn's disease of the colon/ileum/jejunum/duodenum/stomach/esophagus

One Disease, Two, or More?

Some experts in the field have thought that ulcerative colitis and Crohn's disease are merely two forms of the same disease, perhaps because some people who "clearly" have ulcerative colitis "clearly" develop features of Crohn's disease at a later date. It is extremely rare, though, for an expert to diagnose Crohn's colitis, and then change the diagnosis later to ulcerative colitis. It is also extremely rare for both diseases to coexist in one person.

Because we cannot always tell if the problem is ulcerative colitis or Crohn's disease, we tell some patients that they have "indeterminate colitis." This too has encouraged the perception of IBD as just one disease. In many cases, not being able to say which kind of colitis it is doesn't matter. Except when surgery is necessary, most treatments are the same for both ulcerative colitis and Crohn's disease.

Where Does Ulcerative Colitis Occur?

Ulcerative colitis occurs only in the colon. It always involves the rectum. It should be continuous – that is, not confined to patches.

Some patients have inflammation just in the rectum (known as ulcerative proctitis). Others have it in the rectum and the sigmoid colon. Some have it in the rectum, the sigmoid colon, and the descending colon up to the splenic flexure. Others have it from the rectum around into the transverse colon. Some have it as far as the hepatic flexure. Yet others have it throughout the entire colon to the cecum.

Ulcerative colitis involves the rectum plus or minus the sigmoid in 30 percent of cases, approximately the left half to two-thirds of the colon in 40 percent of cases, and the whole colon in 30 percent of cases.

Learning about medicine means accepting the fact that we can never say "never" and we can never say "always." Occasionally there are patients in whom ulcerative colitis is not continuous. What we see then is involvement of the rectum and part of the descending colon, plus a patch in the cecum, usually around the opening into the appendix. The patch near the appendix looks just like ulcerative colitis anywhere else. As you will see, patchy disease is typical of Crohn's disease; however, it is believed that these people with a patch of colitis around the appendix and typical ulcerative colitis elsewhere do in fact have ulcerative colitis.

In some patients with ulcerative colitis, the inner lining of the last few inches (centimeters) of the ileum becomes mildly inflamed. This inflammation is called backwash ileitis; it does not cause any symptoms or problems. We don't know why some patients get backwash ileitis and others don't.

Exactly What Is Inflamed in Ulcerative Colitis?

In ulcerative colitis, inflammation is usually confined to the inner lining of the colon, or *mucosa*. The surface of this inner lining becomes raw and bleeds easily, and looks a lot like scraped skin.

Where Does Crohn's Disease Occur?

Crohn's disease can occur anywhere from the mouth to the anus. Most commonly (45 percent) it occurs in the end of the ileum and the beginning of the colon (cecum plus or minus ascending colon). Next most commonly (35 percent) it occurs just in the end of the ileum. Third most commonly (20 percent) it occurs just in the colon. Here it may be patchy or continuous, and may or may not involve the rectum. In a few patients the jejunum, duodenum, stomach, or esophagus is involved. For most patients with inflammation in these areas, the ileum or the colon or both are involved as well, but in a few people the disease is isolated in one or more of those locations. When Crohn's disease occurs in the mouth, it is almost always associated with Crohn's disease elsewhere in the GI tract.

Exactly What Is Inflamed in Crohn's Disease?

In Crohn's disease, the entire thickness of the bowel wall, from the inner lining (the mucosa) through the muscle layers to the outer lining (the *serosa*), is inflamed. In addition to swelling of the bowel wall, Crohn's disease causes swelling of the *mesentery*, a fan-shaped piece of tissue that connects the small intestine to the back wall of the abdomen and contains the main intestinal blood vessels and lymph glands.

T W O

Who Gets IBD?
What Causes It?

Who Gets IBD?

Inflammatory bowel disease can begin at any age. Most commonly it appears between the ages of 15 and 30 or – less often – between the ages of 45 and 60. It occurs throughout the world, but it is much more prevalent in temperate climates than in tropical ones. It is found more often in developed areas such as North America, the United Kingdom, Scandinavia, and Western Europe than in developing countries. IBD has been very uncommon in Asia, even in the highly developed countries, but has become an increasing problem in Japan. Most studies report that IBD is more likely to occur in people of a higher socioeconomic bracket. However, poorer people are less likely to seek treatment for their disease, so this may skew the studies.

Is IBD More Common in Certain Population Groups?

IBD is a little more common in Jews than in non-Jews. But this applies only to Ashkenazi Jews, who are mostly from Eastern Europe – not to Sephardic Jews, who come from Spain and other Mediterranean countries, or to Asiatic Jews. Furthermore, Crohn's disease is less common in Eastern European

Jews who move to Israel. IBD is much less common in blacks and Asians than in Caucasians. Asians are unlikely to have IBD if they live in the Far East, but develop it more frequently if they move to Western European countries. On the other hand, young Asians who are born in Britain are at a significantly higher risk of developing IBD than the indigenous European population. What all this tells us is that the issue of who gets IBD, and why, is very complicated.

In many parts of the world men and women seem to get ulcerative colitis in equal numbers, but in most places Crohn's disease is slightly more common in women than in men.

How Common Is IBD?
Many studies have been done to estimate the frequency of inflammatory bowel disease. Estimates of the number of cases in North America range from 10 per 100,000 to 1,000 per 100,000.

Is IBD Increasing?
Statistics for ulcerative colitis have not changed significantly of late, but Crohn's disease has been on the increase. Part of the reason is a change in medical thinking about IBD. It was originally thought that Crohn's disease occurred only in the small intestine, while all chronic colitis was ulcerative colitis. In the 1950s and 1960s Crohn's colitis became accepted as a distinct entity. Many people who had originally been told that they had ulcerative colitis were told, "You never had ulcerative colitis. It was Crohn's disease from the start, but we didn't know it at the time." Even so, Crohn's is still on the rise.

What Causes IBD?
We know a lot about IBD, but we don't yet know what causes it. Here are some of the factors that may play a role.

Genes May Predispose You to IBD.
There are several reasons for believing that IBD has a genetic component. It is important to realize that most IBD patients do not have any relatives at all with IBD. But if a person has ulcerative colitis, there is about a 10 percent chance of IBD in other members of the extended family, with ulcerative colitis more likely than Crohn's disease. On the other hand, if a person has Crohn's disease, there is about a 15 to 25 percent chance of IBD in the extended family, with Crohn's disease more likely than ulcerative colitis. If a person has IBD, the risk of that person's child developing IBD is thought to be about 5 percent. Remember that this means the child has about a 95 percent chance of *not* developing IBD. However, if both parents have IBD, the risk of IBD occurring in the children seems to be at least 50 percent.

Studies of identical twins have shown that if one twin develops Crohn's disease, the chance of the other twin developing it is 44 to 58 percent, usually within a few years. If one twin develops ulcerative colitis, however, the probability that the other member will develop ulcerative colitis is much less. There are no reports of one identical twin having ulcerative colitis and the other having Crohn's disease. This tells us that these disorders have a similar but not identical genetic basis.

Within the last few years, human gene research has provided us with some of the most exciting developments in medicine. While little has been accomplished so far in ulcerative colitis, mutations (genetic changes) in a gene known as NOD2 (also known as CARD 15), located on chromosome 16, have been shown to predispose *some* people to Crohn's in the ileum, especially the form of the disease that causes a lot of scarring and narrowing. But NOD2 mutations have been found in only one-quarter to one-third of patients. Interestingly, NOD2 is a member of a family of cell proteins associated with disease-resistance genes in plants.

As well, researchers have identified a group of antibodies known as *antineutrophil cytoplasmic antibodies (ANCA)*, which are present in high levels in many people with ulcerative colitis, and in a significant number of their relatives, even when those relatives do not have IBD. These antibodies are found in low levels in some people with Crohn's disease and a small proportion of their relatives, and are not found at all in healthy families. Another group of antibodies, known as *anti-Saccharomyces cerevisiae antibodies (ASCA)*, are present in high levels in some people with Crohn's disease and in some of their relatives.

Another factor that may be inherited is increased permeability (leakiness) of the intestinal lining in people with Crohn's disease (see "abnormal immunity," below).

Certain diseases occur more commonly in people with IBD. One of the best-known examples is the arthritic disease ankylosing spondylitis (see Chapter 9). Several years ago, Canadian researchers showed an association between multiple sclerosis and Crohn's disease, and it has been known for some time that people with Crohn's disease have a greater chance of having psoriasis. Recent studies suggest that left-handed people are twice as likely to get IBD (either form) as right-handers. Associations such as these support the concept that there is a genetic predisposition to IBD.

While this genetic information is important, we mustn't forget that it's widely accepted that there are environmental risk factors for IBD as well. Genetic research has begun to reveal some of the secrets of IBD, and we can expect more positive results in the future.

Abnormal Immunity May Be a Factor

Chapter 1 outlined the digestive functions of the GI tract. A second function, less well understood, is that of protecting the body against potentially harmful infectious agents or chemical substances.

The inner lining of the intestine (the mucosa) contains many types of immune cells that act as defenders in recognizing foreign substances, known as antigens. These cells prevent such substances from passing through the mucosa and entering the body. Some of these cells, called macrophages, engulf the potentially harmful substances. Other cells, called lymphocytes, produce antibodies — chemical products that bind to and inactivate foreign substances and infectious agents. Sometimes, however, this immune response in the mucosa breaks down, and harmful agents or chemicals penetrate into the deeper layers of the intestine. This produces inflammation. This type of process *may* be important in IBD.

Lymphocytes also produce chemicals known as cytokines. Some lymphocytes produce Th1 cytokines while others make Th2 cytokines. Normally the production of these two types of cytokines is balanced, but research shows that there is an imbalance in IBD: Th1 cytokines are over-produced and Th2 cytokines are under-produced. Many treatments for IBD attempt to rebalance their production. The immunosuppressive drugs used to treat IBD (see Chapter 6) suppress the Th1 lymphocytes. Although this is frequently beneficial, suppressing any part of the immune system can have undesirable side effects. Recent work has focused on *stimulating* the Th2 system instead.

Research also shows that healthy people have an invisible intestinal "barrier" that can prevent various substances from being absorbed. Canadian researchers have demonstrated that this barrier is "leaky" in people with Crohn's disease, so that substances that would not normally be absorbed may be able to enter the intestinal tissues and trigger inflammation.

Numerous researchers have tried to show that IBD is an "autoimmune" disease, meaning that the disease occurs because the body attacks itself. Multiple abnormalities of the immune system have in fact been detected in people with IBD, but many researchers think these abnormalities are a result of the disease, not the cause. Even if these abnormalities perpetuate the disease, the factor that set off the disease in the first place remains the vital unknown.

IBD and Infections

There is no convincing evidence that IBD is due to infection. But infectious colitis (which is caused by bacteria, viruses, or

---

What about Stress?

The issue of stress and the gut is an important one. Many people in the general population (i.e., people who do not have IBD) have gastrointestinal problems when they are under stress, and this has led to an assumption that stress has a role to play in IBD as well. The condition known as irritable bowel syndrome (IBS) is a disorder in which people tend to have abdominal pain and irregular bowel movements without any intestinal inflammation. Many people with IBS have a considerable increase in their symptoms when they are mentally stressed. Everyone is familiar with the term "tension headaches," and people are not embarrassed to talk about them. But you don't hear a lot of people talking about their "tension vomiting" or "tension diarrhea" or "tension bellyaches," although these are every bit as common. As with tension headaches, tension gut symptoms can occur in any pattern, from occasionally to daily.

Doctors used to think that IBD was caused by stress. There is no evidence for this, and it is no longer believed by experts in the field. Controversy still exists, however, about the possible role of stress as a precipitating factor in flare-ups in a person with pre-existing IBD. Even if stress is a factor, it generally cannot be avoided, and the thought that a particular stress may cause a flare-up of the disease is in itself stressful.

People with IBD can also have IBS, and no doubt the occurrence of both conditions in the same person helps to perpetuate the idea that stress causes IBD. The experienced doctor and the experienced IBD patient know that IBD can begin when things are going well or when they are going badly. Saying that IBD is a psychological illness suggests that, because of the kind of person you are, you are in some way responsible for the disease. This is likely to make you feel guilty, which can make you feel even worse. Remember, it's not your fault!

parasites) and ulcerative colitis are similar, and Crohn's disease is strikingly like intestinal tuberculosis (which is caused by a bacterium).

Johne's disease is a Crohn's-like disease that occurs in a large variety of animals, but especially ruminants (such as cows and deer). The cause is a bacterium belonging to the tuberculosis family, known as *Mycobacterium avium*, subspecies *paratuberculosis* (MAP for short, or just *Mycobacterium paratuberculosis*). A group of British researchers has been strongly promoting the idea that Crohn's disease is caused by this bacterium. They believe that milk is the vehicle carrying the infection into the intestine. Despite their enthusiasm, most other experts in the field remain unconvinced, as this idea has been examined repeatedly over the last 25 years, with mostly negative results.

Some research has suggested that certain types of infection may actually be beneficial. One American researcher, Dr. Weinstock, has been treating Crohn's patients by infesting them with a worm! This treatment stimulates Th1 cytokine production. Because IBD is very uncommon in tropical third-world countries with poor sanitation, Dr. Weinstock and his colleagues have proposed that infestation with worms, which is common in such places, may help protect people against IBD.

Smoking Increases the Risk of Getting Crohn's Disease.
Numerous studies conducted since 1987 have demonstrated that cigarette smoking is a risk factor for Crohn's disease. It appears that smoking also increases the likelihood that Crohn's disease will recur after surgery; giving up smoking soon after surgery makes a recurrence less likely. How smoking exerts these effects is unknown. However, the evidence is compelling enough that if you have Crohn's disease and you smoke, you should give it up. In addition, it was recently shown that smoking reduces

your chance of responding to the drug infliximab. Paradoxically, nicotine seems to protect some people against ulcerative colitis! As for second-hand smoke, passive smoking increases the risk of IBD in children. This makes sense in Crohn's disease, which is associated with smoking, but goes contrary to what has been established in ulcerative colitis, where smoking should be protective.

Oral Contraceptives and IBD

Research on IBD among oral-contraceptive users is inconclusive. While the risk of developing IBD seems to be increased, stopping the pill often makes no difference.

Many gastroenterologists (physicians who specialize in treating diseases of the GI tract) consider it worthwhile for women with poorly controlled IBD to stop the pill temporarily to see what happens. If this is not possible, switching to a lower-estrogen pill is an alternative. Because the oral contraceptive remains one of the most effective forms of birth control, women should carefully consider the potential benefits and risks of stopping the pill or avoiding it altogether.

A Blood-Vessel Abnormality May Cause Crohn's Disease.

An old idea, which has recently received renewed attention from an IBD research group in London, England, is that Crohn's disease is due to an inadequate supply of oxygen to one or more parts of the intestine as a result of inflammation and blockage of small blood vessels within the intestine. Experimental studies interfering with blood flow create an appearance that is somewhat similar to Crohn's disease, with areas of inflammation and narrowing of the intestine.

Ulcerative Colitis As a Result of "Malnutrition" of the Colonic Mucosa (Inner Lining)

Compounds known as short-chain fatty acids are essential

nutrients for the mucosa of the colon. These compounds are produced as bacteria break down complex carbohydrate residue (i.e., fiber) in the colon (see Chapter 1). If the colon is deprived of these compounds, the mucosa sometimes becomes inflamed and bleeds easily.

An Australian researcher named Roediger suggested that ulcerative colitis is a nutritional deficiency disease of the colon in which there is an inadequate supply and/or delivery of short-chain fatty acids to the mucosa. Recent research has not supported this hypothesis, despite the fact that selected patients do seem to respond to treatment for such a deficiency.

Odds and Ends
Within the past fifteen years, a growing body of experimental and clinical evidence has suggested that a class of chemicals known as reactive oxygen metabolites may play an important role in the development of IBD. Some of these chemicals are classified as "oxidants"; others are referred to as "free radicals." Some of the drug therapies used in IBD, such as 5-ASA (see Chapter 6), have potent antioxidant activity. However, much more work needs to be done to determine the role of these chemicals.

- Nitric oxide is an important natural chemical involved in many disease processes. Studies are underway to determine if it plays any role in IBD.
- People with ulcerative colitis are much less likely than are members of a comparable control group to have undergone an appendectomy. It appears that appendectomy protects against UC. However, some researchers have suggested that this is only true if the appendix is removed before age 21. Conversely, appendectomy seems to increase the chance of developing Crohn's disease.

ɔm time to time, researchers have tried to link dietary ɪctors to the development of IBD. Milk, corn flakes, a high intake of refined sugar, baker's yeast, and various other dietary constituents have been put forward as risk factors. To date, these theories either have been disproved or have not been conclusively proved. Recently milk has re-entered the picture, but as a vehicle for a tuberculosis-like bacterium (see above).

- It has been suggested that the significant components of food may be not the nutrients themselves, but a variety of inert, inorganic, non-nutrient particles found routinely in our food. These include natural contaminants (soil and dust), food additives, and anti-caking agents. These components may combine with bacterial particles, pass through a defective gut barrier, and provoke inflammation.

So Where Does This Leave Us?
Our current understanding of the development of IBD is as follows. First, you must have a genetically susceptible subject. This person must then come in contact with some agent or substance that, through some defect in the normal intestinal defense system, is able to penetrate the intestinal wall. This sets up an inflammatory response. A defect in regulating the inflammatory response must also exist so that, once the immune system is activated, a complex process is started that the body is unable to stop.

We still have no answer to the question of what causes IBD, but research is ongoing. There is every reason to be optimistic and to believe that the causes of ulcerative colitis and Crohn's disease will eventually be found.

THREE

Symptoms and Signs

S ymptoms are things that you can *feel* and tell your doctor about. Pain, poor appetite, nausea, and diarrhea are common symptoms of IBD. Signs are things that you or your doctor can *observe*. Being pale, having a rash, or passing blood into the toilet are all common signs of IBD. At times symptoms and signs are difficult to separate. If you have an itchy rash, the itch is a symptom and the rash is a sign. A diagnosis is easier to make with both symptoms and signs. This is why your doctor will frequently ask you many questions about a complaint. The more information you give, the more accurate the diagnosis will be, and the better the treatment.

Symptoms of Ulcerative Colitis

The most typical characteristic of ulcerative colitis is bloody diarrhea; bloody diarrhea makes us think of ulcerative colitis and ulcerative colitis makes us think of bloody diarrhea. There are always exceptions, of course. Some people with this condition have bleeding without diarrhea and some even have bleeding with constipation (particularly people with ulcerative proctitis). Mostly, though, it's bloody diarrhea.

Next to that, the most typical symptom of ulcerative colitis is the false urge: you get a feeling that you are going to have bowel movement, but when you get to the toilet nothing or almost nothing comes out. Sometimes there's some gas, or some "wet" gas, or a little blood, or even a bit of stool, but there is no reasonable amount of stool. The total number of trips to the toilet, for actual bowel movements and false urges combined, is one of the indicators of how severe an attack of colitis is.

As a *rough* guide, two to five trips to the toilet in twenty-four hours indicate a mild attack of colitis, five to ten trips indicate a moderate attack, and ten to twenty or thirty trips indicate a severe attack.

Closely related to the false urge is a symptom named *tenesmus*. You experience it as persistent pressure in the region of the anus; it feels like a constant false urge. It is usually not relieved completely (sometimes not at all) by passing gas or fluid or even feces.

Tenesmus is typically due to inflammation and spasm of the rectum. When a normal rectum is filled with stool, it sends a message to the brain that says, "Go to the bathroom and have a bowel movement." A healthy person responds by going to the bathroom, but can also have the brain say to the rectum, "Not now – I'm busy." The rectum will relax and the urge to go the bathroom will disappear. When the rectum is inflamed, however, it is in spasm all the time. A rectum in spasm sends the same message to the brain as a full rectum. You constantly feel you need to go to the bathroom. The rectum does not accept the message "Not now – I'm busy." Even when you sit on the toilet, even if you have a bowel movement, this urge to pass stool is not completely relieved. The reason, of course, is that the rectum is still inflamed and therefore still in spasm, so the message from the rectum to the brain doesn't change very much.

Aside from bloody stools and frequent trips to the toilet, many people with ulcerative colitis experience crampy pain in the abdomen, low down on the left side, across the lower abdomen, or across the upper and lower abdomen. Such pain, often described as squeezing, is usually followed by a trip to the toilet. Typically, the pain is relieved by passing stool or gas, or both.

Other symptoms that may be experienced by people with ulcerative colitis are reduced appetite, weight loss, lack of energy, fever, chills, and sweats. These symptoms are either absent or mild in someone with a mild attack of colitis, but can be dramatic in a severe attack.

Are People with Ulcerative Colitis Sick All the Time?
It is important to recognize that most people with ulcerative colitis are well between attacks. In any given person, attacks, or flare-ups, may occur frequently (every few weeks) or rarely (every few years). A person may have multiple flare-ups one year and then none for several years, or any other irregular pattern that you can imagine. The average risk of a flare-up is about 10 percent per year. A small number of people with ulcerative colitis (about 5 percent) have what is known as chronic continuous colitis.

Signs of Ulcerative Colitis
For most people with ulcerative colitis there are few signs of the disease, other than blood in the stool. In some patients, the doctor can feel a fullness in the right lower quadrant of the abdomen. This is because stool piles up in the ascending colon during an attack. The colon is extremely inefficient at emptying itself when it is inflamed, even though you may go to the bathroom many times.

Symptoms of Crohn's Disease

Crohn's disease is somewhat more complicated than ulcerative colitis because it can affect different parts of the GI tract. The general symptoms are crampy abdominal pain, diarrhea, and weight loss. Pain is most often felt around the navel and/or lower right part of the abdomen. It is often associated with eating, and can begin during a meal, soon after, or within an hour or so. A steady, dull ache in the lower right abdomen may also be felt. It is usually somewhat worse with activity, especially anything that jiggles the abdomen, such as jogging. Crohn's patients also suffer from a lack of energy.

Symptoms of Small-Bowel Crohn's Disease

Some 70 to 80 percent of patients with small-bowel Crohn's disease complain of crampy abdominal pain, diarrhea, and weight loss. Many people quickly learn that they can avoid

---

IBD Lookalikes

Many other medical conditions are characterized by diarrhea and crampy pain, like inflammatory bowel disease. Diagnosing IBD means ruling them out.

- Infections can mimic IBD: food poisoning or traveler's diarrhea (common causes are Campylobacter, Salmonella, E. coli, Shigella), antibiotic-associated colitis (due to Clostridium difficile), yersiniosis, giardiasis, intestinal tuberculosis.
- Irritable bowel syndrome (IBS) can resemble Crohn's disease.
- Foods can cause chronic diarrhea: lactose, if you are lactose intolerant; caffeine; fructose; non-absorbable sugars, such as sorbitol, mannitol, xylitol, maltol, and maltitol; a high-fiber diet.
- Drugs can cause chronic diarrhea: antibiotics, nonsteroidal anti-inflammatory drugs (NSAIDs), chemotherapeutic drugs, and many others.
- Other IBD lookalikes include radiation enteritis after radiation treatment for certain cancers; ischemic (lack of blood flow) disease of the intestine; collagenous and/or microscopic colitis; Behçet's disease.

"They thought I had appendicitis."

Some patients with undiagnosed small-bowel Crohn's become ill suddenly and go to the hospital with severe abdominal pain. The attack is similar to acute appendicitis, and surgery may be necessary to make the correct diagnosis. The appendix is usually removed, whether it is normal or not. This is a good idea for the most part, because any future attacks will not be blamed on appendicitis.

pain by avoiding food, and this is the main reason people lose weight. Occasionally someone with small-bowel Crohn's is troubled by constipation rather than diarrhea.

Is It Crohn's or Is It IBS?

The main alternative diagnosis to Crohn's disease is irritable bowel syndrome (IBS). However, people with IBS rarely lose weight. Early in the onset of symptoms of Crohn's disease there may not be weight loss, and this may delay the correct diagnosis. Here's a case in point.

A 21-year-old woman developed crampy pain around her navel and mild diarrhea with three to four mushy bowel movements a day. The crampy pain and diarrhea came mainly after meals. She was otherwise well and had never been sick before. She thought she might have "the flu." When the symptoms persisted for two weeks and became slightly worse, she went to see her family doctor. He examined her abdomen, said it was normal, and told her she probably had irritable bowel syndrome. No X-rays or blood tests were performed. The woman was reassured that nothing serious was wrong and was told there was nothing to be done for these mild symptoms.

Four weeks later the symptoms were still present and somewhat worse. The woman was now having four to six bowel movements a day, and occasionally got up at night to have them. She had lost ten pounds (almost five kilograms). She decided to go see her mother's family doctor. The physical examination, blood tests, and an X-ray of the colon were normal. Again she was told that she probably had irritable bowel syndrome. When asked if she was nervous, she said that she was. (Anyone having cramps in the abdomen and unpredictable diarrhea for six weeks is bound to be a little nervous!) She was offered a tranquilizer. She tried it, but it just made her feel dopey and did not change her symptoms.

Four more weeks passed. By this time she had lost twenty pounds. She went back to her own doctor. He arranged for a small-bowel X-ray which revealed Crohn's disease in the ileum. The woman was promptly referred to a gastroenterologist and treatment was started, with good results.

In the past, this was a very common sequence of events. Statistics in the 1970s indicated that the average time it took, from the point when someone began complaining until the diagnosis of Crohn's disease was made, was three years. Since some people were diagnosed quickly, this means that in other people the delay was much longer. Over the past thirty years, much more attention has been given to IBD in medical schools. As a result, doctors now think of it sooner, make the diagnosis more quickly, and start treatment faster. In many cases, this prevents the person from losing a lot of weight and becoming seriously ill.

Symptoms of Crohn's Disease of the Colon (Crohn's Colitis)
The symptoms of Crohn's colitis are variable, depending on whether the disease occurs in the right side of the colon, the left side, or the whole colon, and whether the rectum is involved. If the disease is primarily on the right side, you will have mainly cramps and diarrhea. If the disease is primarily

on the left side or involves most of the colon, you will likely have cramps, diarrhea, and some blood in the stool. If the rectum is involved, you will have symptoms similar to ulcerative colitis, with false urges (see symptoms of ulcerative colitis in this chapter).

Symptoms of Crohn's Disease of the Ileum and Colon

If you have both small-bowel and large-bowel disease, you may experience symptoms of the disease from either location, or both. Crohn's of the ileum can flare up when the colonic disease is quiet, and vice versa.

Symptoms of Crohn's Disease of the Stomach and/or Duodenum

Many people with Crohn's disease in this part of the GI system have no symptoms, and the inflammation is discovered by chance. Of those who do have symptoms, over 90 percent have pain or discomfort in the upper abdomen (right side, middle, or left side) that comes on during and soon after meals. Nausea, vomiting, or both occur in about 30 percent of patients. Weight loss occurs in over 50 percent of people with symptoms as a result of the tendency to eat less in order to avoid the symptoms. Occasionally, Crohn's disease of the duodenum will mimic ordinary duodenal ulcer disease. In this situation, pain is more likely to occur when you have not eaten for a few hours, and the pain will be relieved by food.

In some people, Crohn's disease of the stomach and/or duodenum produces enough scarring that the outlet of the stomach into the duodenum, or the duodenum itself, becomes progressively narrower. You will be unable to eat a normal-sized meal, and you will have nausea, a prolonged full or bloated feeling in the upper abdomen after meals, and, often, a decrease in appetite.

Symptoms of Crohn's Disease of the Esophagus

This is so rare a form of Crohn's disease that it is not possible to say what the typical symptoms are. Most people are likely to experience chest pain behind the breastbone, usually when they swallow.

Symptoms of Crohn's Disease of the Appendix

Appendicitis due to Crohn's disease may precede symptoms of Crohn's disease elsewhere in the gastrointestinal tract. However, Crohn's disease of the appendix can be present without symptoms in someone who has symptoms of Crohn's disease elsewhere.

As with garden-variety appendicitis, the usual symptom is a sudden onset of pain low down on the right side of the abdomen. Slow healing or development of a fistula (an abnormal connection between two organs) is a clue.

Are People with Crohn's Disease Sick All the Time?

People with Crohn's disease are more likely than those with ulcerative colitis to experience persistent symptoms between flare-ups. But many people are ill only intermittently. As with ulcerative colitis, attacks may occur every few weeks, months, or years. A person may have multiple flare-ups in one year and then none for several years, or any other irregular pattern that you can imagine. The average risk of a flare-up is about 30 percent per year.

Signs of Crohn's Disease

Unlike those with ulcerative colitis, many people with Crohn's have specific signs that, together with the symptoms, point quite strongly to the disease. About 25 percent have an easily felt area of swelling, most commonly in the lower right part of the abdomen. This is much more distinct than the vague fullness that can be felt in some people with ulcerative colitis. The swelling is often the size of a small grapefruit, and often as firm. The area is usually tender, and the tenderness can be anything from mild to extreme. If it is mild, the swelling is usually the result of inflamed intestine and surrounding tissues and enlarged lymph glands. If there is a marked tenderness, the swelling is usually due to a large abscess (boil). In this case the overlying skin may be red, and it may look stretched. In some people, generally those with moderate tenderness, the swelling is due to a combination of swollen tissues and an abscess. In someone thin, the swelling in the abdomen may be visible.

Another common sign of Crohn's disease is peri-anal disease (disease around the anus). This occurs in about 25 percent of cases and usually takes the form of a fistula, with or without one or more abscesses. Some people have very swollen tags of skin around the anus. This finding is quite characteristic of Crohn's disease. Many healthy people who develop hemorrhoids get skin tags, but swelling of these tags is minimal.

F O U R

How Is IBD Diagnosed?

Physicians have an arsenal of tools to aid them in diagnosing inflammatory bowel disease.

Ulcerative Colitis

Ulcerative colitis is diagnosed from symptoms – frequent, urgent trips to the bathroom and bloody diarrhea – and the typically raw or scraped appearance of the rectum when the doctor examines it with an endoscope. During the examination of the rectum, the doctor will usually take a biopsy (tissue sample) to confirm the diagnosis. He or she may also arrange to have stools sent to a lab to check for infections that mimic ulcerative colitis.

Sigmoidoscopy

Usually a patient suspected of having ulcerative colitis will undergo a sigmoidoscopy or flexible sigmoidoscopy ("-oscopy" means to look into; to look into the sigmoid colon is sigmoidoscopy). This involves passing an instrument (a sigmoidoscope) through the anus into the rectum, and then into the sigmoid colon. The procedure allows the physician to view the mucosa (inner lining) of the bowel.

Colonoscopy
In a colonoscopy (looking into the colon), the doctor examines most or all of the colon. It can be used to diagnose IBD and to determine how much of the colon is inflamed. During the procedure, the end of the ileum can also be examined in most people. Colonoscopy can be used, as well, to check for precancerous conditions or cancer itself (see Chapter 10). The procedure is usually done on an outpatient basis. Even if you have diarrhea, the colon needs to be cleaned out for colonoscopy. Sedation is often given to relax you and minimize discomfort.

Preparation for Colonoscopy
The three most commonly used preparations are electrolyte solutions, sodium phosphate solutions, and magnesium citrate. All can cause nausea, vomiting, abdominal fullness, and crampy abdominal pain. Occasionally, these side effects are so severe that the person is unable to continue taking the preparation. Through trial and error, most people find at least one preparation that they can tolerate. Additional information on two of these agents can be found in Chapter 6.

Air-Contrast Barium Enema
Until colonoscopy became widely available, most people with ulcerative colitis had the extent of their disease estimated with an air-contrast barium enema, which is an X-ray of the colon. After the bowel has been appropriately cleansed, a short plastic tube is inserted into the rectum through the anus. Air and a suspension of barium sulfate (an inert substance easily visible on X-rays) are blown into the colon and multiple pictures are taken. Using a bit of barium and a lot of air, the radiologist (a physician specializing in interpreting X-rays) can usually coat the entire lining of the colon. The technique shows details of the inner lining of the colon, which is irregular instead of smooth in people with colitis.

Barium enemas are still commonly used. Family doctors who suspect ulcerative colitis may send you for one. A gastro-enterologist or surgeon may also want you to undergo a barium enema. In some people it is not possible, for technical reasons, to pass the colonoscope all the way around the colon. In others, strictures (areas of narrowing) may prevent passage of the instrument.

Crohn's Disease

Crohn's disease is suspected when a person suffers abdominal cramps and diarrhea, with weight loss, for more than two weeks. A mass of swollen tissue that can be felt in the abdomen strongly increases the doctor's suspicion. Abscesses or fistulas around the anus are even stronger indicators.

Crohn's disease is diagnosed on the basis of X-rays more often than is ulcerative colitis. This is because most Crohn's disease is less accessible by colonoscope than is ulcerative colitis. Most Crohn's disease occurs in the ileum, or the ileum and the right side of the colon. It is neither practical nor pos-sible to do a colonoscopy on every person suspected of having the disease. But someone with chronic diarrhea will very likely have a sigmoidoscopy as part of the investigation.

There are three ways to use X-rays to diagnose Crohn's disease in the ileum.

Small-Bowel Series or Small-Bowel Follow-Through

The first method is a small-bowel series or a small-bowel follow-through (sometimes called a GI motor meal). You are given two or three large glasses of barium-sulfate suspension to drink. As the stomach empties the barium into the small intestine, X-rays are taken at set intervals until the barium arrives at the end of the ileum. At that time, the radiologist usually takes pictures of the end of the ileum. In most people with Crohn's of the ileum, the disease is obvious.

Small-Bowel Enema

The second method is a small-bowel enema. A tube is passed through your nose, down the esophagus, through the stomach into the duodenum and then the jejunum (upper small bowel). Barium is injected through the tube by the radiologist and monitored as it progresses through the small bowel. The main advantage of this technique is that the pictures are sometimes more accurate than a small-bowel series. However, many people dislike the procedure intensely because of the tube. Some radiologists make the experience less uncomfortable by putting freezing in your nose before inserting the tube. Some also give intravenous medication to relax you.

Single-Contrast Barium Enema

The third method, used much less than in the past, is a single-contrast barium enema. This is like an air-contrast barium enema except that no air is used. Barium is run through the anus and rectum, then up the colon to the ileocecal valve (see Chapter 1) and into the end of the ileum.

Is Colonoscopy Used to Diagnose Crohn's Disease?

Abnormalities in the ileum can be missed with X-rays. In selected patients, colonoscopy is performed, passing the colonoscope all the way around the colon and into the ileum. Occasionally, Crohn's disease is diagnosed in this way even when an apparently normal ileum is clearly seen on X-rays. Some gastroenterologists prefer to *start* with colonoscopy in diagnosing Crohn's disease, then proceed to X-rays later, if necessary.

Crohn's disease of the colon can be diagnosed with sigmoidoscopy, colonoscopy, or barium enema.

Enteroscopy

Crohn's disease of the jejunum is generally diagnosed by a small-bowel series or a small-bowel enema. Occasionally, a procedure known as enteroscopy is used to examine the jejunum directly. Your nose and throat are frozen with a spray, intravenous sedation is given, and a scope is passed down the esophagus, through the stomach, and into the small bowel to make or possibly exclude a diagnosis of Crohn's disease. While enteroscopy is useful, most examinations enable us to visualize only the first three to four feet (about a meter) of the jejunum, and most small-bowel Crohn's is in the ileum.

Capsule Endoscopy

This new method for examining the small intestine has generated much excitement. You swallow a capsule about the size of a large vitamin pill. Through computer technology, images of the inner surface (mucosa) of the small intestine are transmitted and recorded. So far, the main application of this test has been to look for obscure causes of gastrointestinal bleeding. It can also be used to see Crohn's disease, and occasionally it finds Crohn's disease that is not demonstrable by other methods. Risks are few, but the capsule can get stuck at a stricture, causing obstruction, which can lead to emergency surgery. The test is very expensive, and it's unnecessary in most people with Crohn's. It is not very useful for examining the colon.

Esophagogastroduodenoscopy

Crohn's disease of the esophagus, stomach, or duodenum is generally diagnosed by an esophagogastroduodenoscopy. This procedure involves passing a scope into the mouth and down the throat after appropriate freezing and/or sedation. Often referred to as OGD or EGD, the procedure is generally painless, or nearly so. Biopsies, which you don't feel, may be taken. Sedation is given to relax you if you are anxious about the procedure, and you may fall asleep, but this is *not* a general anesthetic.

Upper GI Series

Occasionally, Crohn's disease of the esophagus, stomach, or duodenum will be diagnosed with a barium X-ray known as an upper GI series. You drink a barium-sulfate suspension (generally flavored, which helps a little!), and a radiologist takes pictures.

Ultrasound

Although using sound waves (ultrasound) to examine the bowel does not allow a specific diagnosis to be made, it can sometimes show thickened bowel when someone is too ill to undergo routine diagnostic testing. Thickened bowel has several causes, but one of the more common ones is Crohn's disease. Ultrasound can also be used to diagnose certain complications of IBD, especially abscesses and fistulas within the abdomen or pelvis.

CAT (CT) Scan

CAT stands for "computerized axial tomography." Tomography is an X-ray technique whereby pictures of slices of your body are taken without slicing you up! The X-ray machine is controlled by a computer, and axial means that the X-rays are taken along the long axis of your body. A CAT scan of the abdomen starts with a slice across your body at the lower ribs and proceeds downward to your groin. CAT scans can show where the bowel is thick and, sometimes, where it is narrow. The main value of a CAT scan in IBD is that it shows the presence and location of the abscesses and fistulas that occur as a complication of Crohn's disease (see Chapter 9).

Which Is Better – Ultrasound or a CAT Scan?

Ultrasound is believed to be perfectly safe. A CAT scan involves radiation. Generally speaking, ultrasound works better in thin people and CAT scans work better in overweight people. Fat has a distinctive appearance on a CAT scan and can outline various organs and structures. Gas in the bowel can greatly interfere with the transmission of sound waves, so if a patient has a bowel obstruction, or some other reason for having a lot of gas in the bowel, a CAT scan will be better.

Magnetic Resonance Imaging (MR, MRI)

This technology has proven useful in assessing some people with Crohn's disease, especially those with abscesses and/or fistulas. *MR enteroclysis*, a method of examining the small intestine, is still in development, and its place in the evaluation of Crohn's is not fully established. One of the attractions of MR is its safety for most people. But there are serious risks in certain people; you should be asked to complete a questionnaire before the test is booked, to determine whether you are at any risk.

Leukocyte (White Blood Cell) Scan

This test shows areas of intestinal inflammation by picking up concentrations of white blood cells. A small sample of your blood is removed and mixed with a tiny amount of a radioactive substance. The blood is injected back into you and a special camera moves back and forth over your abdomen, taking a kind of picture. It doesn't hurt, and there are no risks. The test is popular in some centers, particularly for children. However, it is not specific for Crohn's disease, and has no advantages over other methods of diagnosis in the vast majority of cases.

FIVE

Diet and IBD

Once the diagnosis of inflammatory bowel disease has been confirmed through tests, and other diseases have been ruled out, the question is how to treat it.

One of the areas of greatest interest to people with IBD is diet. They often experiment with changes in diet, sometimes even before they have received medical advice. People with Crohn's disease often discover that they feel better if they don't eat. Unfortunately this worsens the weight loss many people experience. Some mistakenly believe that spicy or greasy food should be avoided, but then their diet becomes boring. This can lead to eating even less food and losing more weight.

When someone is ill and needs drugs and/or surgery, sometimes maintaining adequate nutrition becomes an afterthought. But good nutrition is always desirable for those with IBD, as it is for everyone. Knowing what good nutrition means is important. If your doctor can't answer all your food-related questions, you can get advice from a dietitian. Be aware that in some countries the term "nutritionist" can be used by anyone; ask your doctor to refer you to someone who is properly trained.

Most people with IBD can eat a perfectly normal or near-normal diet most of the time. But when you are ill, sometimes avoiding certain foods is recommended, or a liquid diet is prescribed.

Common Dietary Restrictions in IBD

Lactose

Lactose is a sugar in dairy products, and is commonly known as "milk sugar." Some people with IBD have less pain, diarrhea, and gas if they restrict lactose in their diet.

In the inner lining of the small intestine, we all have a variety of enzymes (proteins that digest – break down – other chemicals). One of these enzymes is named lactase, and its function is to digest lactose. When lactose is acted on by lactase, it is broken down into two simpler sugars: glucose and galactose.

Lactose Intolerance

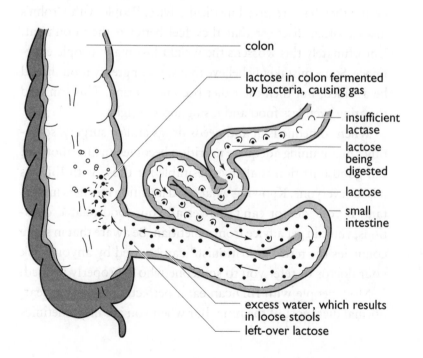

colon

lactose in colon fermented by bacteria, causing gas

insufficient lactase

lactose being digested

lactose

small intestine

excess water, which results in loose stools

left-over lactose

Both are rapidly and easily absorbed through the small intestine into the bloodstream.

As long as you have enough lactase enzyme for the lactose you take in, there is no problem. All the lactose will be digested, and the resulting glucose and galactose will be absorbed. But if you don't produce enough lactase, only some of the lactose will be digested. As the undigested lactose travels down the small intestine, it causes water to be drawn into the intestine by osmosis. This water is held in the intestine and may produce cramps. The extra fluid in the intestine may also cause loose bowel movements (diarrhea).

When this undigested lactose reaches the colon, it *is* digested, but by the bacteria we all have there. The process is known as fermentation. When lactose is fermented by bacteria, it is broken down into an acid and lots of gas. The gas can cause a bloated feeling, pain in the abdomen, and an excess passage of gas from the rectum. The acid can cause anal burning.

What Is Lactose Intolerance?

The symptoms – bloating, pain, diarrhea, gas – that result from a failure to digest lactose are referred to collectively as "lactose intolerance." Some people use the term "lactase deficiency." It really doesn't matter which term you use. The fact is that if you ingest more lactose than your small intestine can handle, you will have some or all of these symptoms.

Who Gets Lactose Intolerance?

As we get older we gradually lose some of our lactase enzyme, and thus are less able to process lactose-containing food. This doesn't happen to everyone, but it happens to many people. It is not serious; it is a nuisance. Of course it's unpleasant to have abdominal pain, diarrhea, or a lot of gas, but it's important to remember that, in this case, it's not dangerous.

Are You Lactose Intolerant?

Some doctors diagnose lactose intolerance by doing a lactose tolerance test. The most practical and direct way to determine lactose intolerance is to vary the amount of lactose in the diet.

Let's compare a couple of examples.

A young woman developed ulcerative colitis. She was treated with medication but was also told to avoid all milk and milk products. Her disease came under good control. She was advised to stay on the low-lactose diet indefinitely. She consulted another gastroenterologist, because she was unhappy about having to avoid dairy products, and was told she should gradually increase her intake of milk and milk products. She was able to resume her usual habit of a glass of milk a day and cheese three to four times a week. There was no evidence of lactose intolerance.

A middle-aged man was referred to a physician for a second opinion because he had persistent diarrhea with his Crohn's disease despite taking several medications. He said he had never tried any dietary restriction. He was in the habit of having cold cereal with milk every morning, cheese two or three times a week in a sandwich, yogurt occasionally, and ice cream frequently in the summer. He was advised to stop all milk, cheese, yogurt, and ice cream for one week, then report back. Prior to restricting his intake of lactose, he was having five to ten watery bowel movements a day with an excessive amount of gas. One week later he reported that he was having three to five bowel movements a day with much less gas. Because of this improvement, he was referred to a dietitian for advice on a strict lactose-free diet. Two weeks later, he was having one or two normal bowel movements a day. Clearly he was made completely better by eliminating lactose from his diet.

Lactose intolerance is more common in those of African and Asian descent than in Caucasians. As mentioned in Chapter 2, IBD is more common in Jews than in non-Jews. As it happens, lactose intolerance is also more common in Jews than in certain other ethnic groups. Lactose intolerance can occur in conjunction with IBD, but it is not the cause of IBD. It is also not an allergy. There is some evidence that lactose intolerance may be a little more common in people with IBD than in other people, but this is not definite.

People who are not known to have lactose intolerance *may* experience it for the first time at the onset of their disease. It is worthwhile to avoid lactose to see if it makes a difference. If it does not, then there is no point in avoiding it, because dairy products are a good source of nutrients and energy, and both are important when you are ill.

Remember that you cannot harm yourself by eating lactose-containing foods when you are ill with IBD, even if you have lactose intolerance. You may go to the bathroom more, you may have more abdominal discomfort, and you may have more gas, but this does not mean your disease has gotten worse. Obviously it may be difficult to tell what is going on if this happens, however, and the simple solution is to remove lactose from your diet temporarily.

Maintaining a Good Calcium Intake If You Are Lactose Intolerant

If you restrict the amount of lactose you take in, you may not get enough calcium, vitamin D, protein, and energy. There are ways to have dairy products but avoid most or all lactose.

- Buy lactose-reduced milk and ice cream. Pure lactase enzyme can be added to these at the dairy. This enzyme predigests much of the lactose. Some people find that the milk and ice cream taste a little sweeter than normal, but few have any trouble getting used to them.
- Add lactase to milk yourself, and take lactase tablets just before and while eating foods containing lactose. Lactase enzyme is commercially available in both liquid and tablet form. The liquid form can be added to milk or yogurt, but needs 24 hours to reduce the lactose content. Tablets must be taken with the food. The tablets are

---

"Hidden" Lactose

Many foods contain lactose but are not so labeled. A typical example is processed meat. Lactose is a cheap filler and is used liberally in hot dogs, for instance, to make them larger. Whey may be listed as an ingredient—it contains lactose, which may not be listed. Commercial gravies usually contain lactose because it can increase the volume of the gravy considerably. Interestingly, most breads are made with milk. One way to avoid them is to buy bread at a kosher Jewish bakery, where milk is not used in preparing bread. As well, many pills contain lactose. People with a marked lactose intolerance may experience symptoms if they take them.

---

especially handy when you are eating in a restaurant, as you may not know which foods contain dairy products or added lactose.

- Eat aged cheeses. Aging cheese reduces the amount of lactose in it because aging involves adding bacteria to cause fermentation. "Old" cheddar contains very little lactose and can be eaten comfortably by most people with lactose intolerance. Those with mild lactose intolerance can generally eat cheeses that are less aged, such as medium cheddar.

- Eat yogurt made with live bacterial culture. All yogurt is made with bacteria, but labeling identifies those with live (active) bacteria. The bacteria used produce lactase enzyme and release it. Thus at least some of the lactose in the yogurt can be digested.

Do You Need Extra Calcium If You Are Lactose Intolerant?
If you're trying a low-lactose diet, there is no urgency about taking calcium pills. The body can easily do without the lost calcium for weeks, even months. In fact, many healthy adults have relatively little calcium in their diet, and in some people it doesn't make much difference. The body controls the blood calcium level the way a thermostat controls the temperature

Although people often talk about the "calories" in food, the scientifically correct term is "kilocalories" (there are 1,000 calories in a kilocalorie, or Kcal; the metric equivalent is 4.184 kilojoules). Because of this confusion, I prefer to use the term "energy" when I am discussing caloric intake in a general sense. Where specific Kcal values are given, they are the same as the so-called "calories" popularly referred to in dieting books and articles.

in a house. If the blood calcium level is a little low, then the body extracts calcium from the bones. Of course, this can make the bones soft and more prone to fracture. But other factors influence the strength of the bones, such as exercise, the amount of vitamin D in the diet, and exposure to sunlight, which leads to the formation of extra vitamin D in the skin.

Many adults develop osteoporosis as they get older. The use of glucocorticosteroids (often called steroids) such as prednisone to treat IBD increases the risk. It is well recognized that calcium can be added to the skeleton easily up to the age of 35. After 35 it becomes more difficult. Providing enough calcium to prevent further deterioration seems to be effective, although medications may also be needed to treat osteoporosis.

Once you have established what level of lactose you can tolerate, having a registered dietitian assess the amount of calcium in your diet is useful.

Should You Take Calcium Pills?

If your calcium intake is below the recommended daily amount, you can improve your intake, either by changing your diet or by taking calcium tablets. If you are going to take calcium tablets, tell your doctor. Calcium is absorbed more effectively in the presence of vitamin D. You can buy a calcium–vitamin D tablet. If you can't find a combined tablet that gives you the amount of calcium you need, you can buy calcium tablets alone and take the cheapest daily multivitamin pill to get the vitamin D you need. Remember that both vitamin D and calcium can be bad for you, as well as good for you. Too much of either one can make you seriously ill. Just because a little vitamin D is needed to help absorb calcium doesn't mean that a lot is better for you. Discuss this with your doctor.

Some people get constipated on calcium and this may mean the dose has to be reduced. Taking excessive calcium can lead to kidney stones, and even calcium deposits in various organs and tissues, sometimes with serious results.

Numerous calcium tablets are available on the market. Some are "name brand"; many sold in large chain pharmacies are "house brand"; and there are others. Using calcium that comes from oyster shells has become popular. This is perfectly all right provided the product is reputable. Name-brand and house-brand tablets are generally acceptable. But you should know that oyster shells can be contaminated with undesirable elements such as arsenic.

Some people take bone-meal tablets. These are made from horse bones, some of which contain a lot of lead. Such tablets are *not* an advisable source of calcium.

What about "Roughage" or Fiber?

Fruit, vegetables, and grains are considered essential ingredients of a healthy, well-balanced diet.

Some of these foods have a laxative effect, and clearly this is undesirable when you are in the midst of a flare-up of IBD. These foods can also produce excessive gas, which may be particularly bothersome during a flare-up.

Two chemicals in fruit are likely to act as laxatives – sorbitol and fructose. Sorbitol is present primarily in prunes, peaches, pears, and apple juice. It is also used as a sweetener in many kinds of gum, in some mints, and in some liquid medications. We are unable to digest sorbitol, and have a limited ability to absorb fructose. We can handle some of either one without getting a laxative effect, but if an excess (which differs for different people) of one or both is taken in, then it acts just like lactose in a person with lactose intolerance. Like unabsorbed lactose, both cause water to be drawn into the intestine by osmosis and this leads to loose stools. And just like unabsorbed lactose, both are broken down in the colon by bacteria, releasing excessive gas. In addition to sorbitol, many gums, candies, and other processed foods contain one or more of the following sugars – mannitol, xylitol, maltol, and maltitol – which can have the same effects as sorbitol.

Many vegetables and grains are a "natural" source of gas. The gas is produced when bacteria digest complex-carbohydrate residue in the colon. An enzyme product called Beano can predigest the fiber in these foods before it reaches the colon. The breakdown products do not include gas. Beano may be effective in reducing gas from peas and beans, nuts and seeds, grains and cereals, and a variety of vegetables. (A detailed list is available from the manufacturer.) Beano is used by mixing a few drops in with those foods that may produce gas, or by taking tablets with your meals. It is available in most pharmacies. People who are allergic to penicillin may also be allergic to Beano, because it is taken from a mold, just like penicillin.

Someone having a flare-up of IBD may well be more comfortable avoiding fruits and vegetables. Many people with IBD can return to eating these foods between flare-ups. However, others always have a degree of diarrhea and recognize that they are better off without these foods, good as they may be.

It is perfectly all right to experiment with different fruits and vegetables to see if you tolerate some better than others. Some people know that they have to avoid foods that contain sorbitol but that they will have no difficulty with other fruit, such as some berries.

People who have small-bowel Crohn's with a narrowing (stricture) in the small intestine may have particular difficulty with fibrous foods, because the stricture is fixed in size and cannot get wider, no matter how hard the intestine tries to push fibrous foods through. These people may get crampy pain when they eat some fruits and vegetables.

Cereal fiber, such as bran, may not cause a problem for small-bowel Crohn's patients because bran can change shape and be squeezed through the narrowed areas. Bran may have to be avoided, though, because it is a potent laxative. It also produces troublesome gas in some cases.

Restricting fruits and vegetables necessarily means a decreased intake of minerals (potassium and iron) and vitamins (A, C, and folic acid). The solutions are to eat bananas (potassium); increase citrus juices, tomato juice, ketchup, and brown sugar (potassium, vitamin C); increase meat (iron and folic acid); increase milk and milk products (if you are not lactose intolerant) and liver (vitamin A); eat whole-grain cereals (fiber); and avoid only coarse fibers (celery, apple skins) and large seeds.

What about Meat?
Some people with IBD think they feel better if they avoid meat. Certain bacteria in the colon act on meat residues and produce hydrogen sulfide gas. There is some evidence that this is bad for the health of the cells in the lining of the colon, and that this may be a factor in aggravating colitis. But this is controversial, and meat is a good source of protein and iron.

Fat

Some patients with small-bowel Crohn's disease do have to reduce the amount of fat in their diet, if the last three feet (about a meter) or more of the ileum is severely diseased, or has been surgically removed or bypassed (see Chapter 7). Fat absorption is very likely to be decreased and diarrhea will result or, if already present, will likely be aggravated. This results in a loss of energy intake (and probably a loss of weight).

How Can a Patient on a Low-Fat Diet Compensate?

If you are on a low-fat diet, can maintain an acceptable weight, and are not bothered by the fat restriction, there is nothing you need do. But if you need to gain weight, or you would like to use fat for salad dressing or cooking, there is a manufactured food product you can use. It is known as MCT, which stands for "medium-chain triglyceride." Many nutritional products contain MCTs, but there are only two products in which MCTs make up all or most of the fat.

The first is MCT oil. This is a pure liquid oil product derived from coconut oil. Many people take it as they would any liquid medication. It can also be mixed with fruit juices, used on salads and other vegetables, incorporated into sauces, or used in other cooking and baking. One tablespoon (15mL) provides 115 kilocalories. The second product comes as a powder and must be mixed with water prior to use.

Individuals with advanced cirrhosis of the liver must use these products with caution because large amounts can cause drowsiness or confusion.

Clear Fluid Diets

Sometimes it is necessary to avoid all food except for clear fluids. In certain situations this can improve your symptoms

A Typical Clear Fluid Diet

Breakfast	Lunch	Dinner
jelly	jelly	jelly
apple juice	apple juice	apple juice
tea with sugar	chicken broth	beef broth
	tea with sugar	tea with sugar

dramatically – particularly if you have small-bowel Crohn's disease and especially if the symptoms are due to a partial small-bowel obstruction.

If you are in hospital and have not been allowed to eat or drink *anything*, clear fluids are wonderful, even enjoyable for a day or two. After that, this diet gets pretty boring, not to mention that it is very poor nutritionally. It supplies only 400 to 600 kilocalories (1,700 to 2,500 kilojoules) per day, with about 135 grams of carbohydrate, 8 grams of protein, and no fat. A person weighing 150 pounds (about 70 kilos) needs at least 1,500 kilocalories (6,300 kilojoules), 60 grams of protein, and a small amount of fat each day. So it is important for both you and your doctor to remember that you should not be on clear fluids for more than a few days, unless there's no choice.

Full Fluid Diets

A patient doing well on a clear fluid diet may move to a full fluid diet. A typical full fluid diet provides 1,100 to 1,300 kilocalories (4,600 to 5,400 kilojoules) a day, and usually contains at least 165 grams of carbohydrate, 40 grams of protein, and an equivalent amount of fat. If lactose intolerance is not a problem, this diet is certainly a great improvement over a clear fluid diet, though it does not include enough energy or protein for most people recovering from an illness or an operation. If you are lactose intolerant, a full fluid diet cannot be used, since many of the

A Typical Full Fluid Diet

Breakfast	Lunch	Dinner
orange juice	blended juice	pineapple juice
strained oatmeal	strained cream soup	strained cream soup
2% milk	custard	ice cream
brown sugar	2% milk	2% milk
coffee or tea with	coffee or tea with	coffee or tea with
sugar and cream	sugar and cream	sugar and cream

foods in it contain dairy products. In fact, if you subtract the dairy products from the full fluid diet, you are pretty well back to clear fluids. Furthermore, a lot of older people don't like sugar and don't like milk products. This is important to remember, because older people are more vulnerable to various illnesses and complications, especially if they are malnourished.

Why Restrict All Solids?
The purpose of restricting solids is to eliminate most residue (indigestible matter). This is important for people with small-bowel Crohn's disease with partial obstruction or an acute flare-up, but also for some people with fistulas (due to Crohn's disease or as a complication of surgery) or people with short-bowel syndrome (see TPN, below). But as we've seen, restricting solids in the diet results in an inadequate intake of energy and some nutrients.

Elemental Diets, Polymeric Diets, and Modular Products
In the past thirty years a wide range of specialized nutritional products has been developed to insure adequate nutrition for people on fluids.

An "elemental diet" is one in which all nutrients are in their simplest forms. The carbohydrate is present as glucose; the protein is present as amino acids; any fat that is present (usually very little) is in the form of long-chain or medium-chain triglycerides. These components are mixed with all the necessary vitamins, minerals, and trace elements. In concept, the elemental diet is "predigested." In reality, however, the fat supplied requires some digestion. These products are generally available in a powdered form and must be dissolved in water and used within forty-eight hours.

"Polymeric diets" contain complex chemical forms of the various nutrients. For example, carbohydrate may be present in the form of corn syrup; protein is often in the form of casein (this is milk protein – it has nothing to do with lactose); and fat may be in the form of corn oil. Other ingredients may be added to make these diets more palatable. Most of these products are marketed in liquid form in cans or boxes. A few of the polymeric diets are very low in fat. Some come in powdered form and must be mixed with water before use. The canned or boxed products generally have a shelf life of approximately two years. However, once a can or a box has been opened it must be refrigerated and completely used within 48 hours. The majority of these products are lactose-free.

"Modular products" supply one particular nutrient. The medium-chain triglyceride (MCT) product to replace fat is an example of a modular product.

When Are Liquid Diets Used in IBD?

- *Ulcerative colitis:* There are times when someone with ulcerative colitis does not feel like eating much but is willing to drink. Since most ordinary fluids are filling without supplying a lot of energy, liquid diet products can prove very useful. It is also possible to have high-energy, nutritious liquids that are not manufactured. The two best examples are milkshakes and eggnog; they are high in both energy and protein. However, because they also contain a lot of lactose, some people with lactose intolerance cannot use them. If someone with ulcerative colitis can eat a reasonably normal diet, there is no advantage to using specialized products. Nutritional therapy alone is not a treatment for ulcerative colitis.

- *Crohn's disease:* Unlike ulcerative colitis, nutritional therapy alone is an effective treatment for Crohn's disease, especially when the disease is active in the small bowel. In adults, these diets are most often used by patients who want to avoid using steroids to treat the problem, by doctors who want their patients to avoid steroids, or by people who want to stop using steroids but have been unable to do so. Most people who go on a liquid diet will be able to reduce steroids without having a flare-up. A substantial number will be able either to stay off steroids or to use a reduced dose when the liquid-diet course is finished and a regular diet has been resumed. Although it was initially thought that the diet had to be elemental, it has been conclusively shown that polymeric diets are just as good. There is still some controversy about whether all polymeric diets are equally effective. Liquid-diet therapy is almost as effective as prednisone, the steroid most commonly used for Crohn's disease.

About Steroids

The term "steroids" is commonly used to refer to a large number of hormones that have similar chemical structure. They include glucocorticoid steroids (which can reduce inflammation), male sex hormones (such as the so-called anabolic steroids sometimes misused by athletes), female sex hormones, and others.

In this book the term "steroids" refers exclusively to glucocorticoid steroids.

How Do Liquid-Diet Products Work?

So far, we don't know exactly why this type of therapy works. Since these products are sterilized and most regular food is not, many researchers think that certain components of bacteria aggravate the inflammation of Crohn's disease. There is also some evidence that simply making sure you are properly nourished can be beneficial for Crohn's disease.

Does Liquid-Diet Therapy Work for Everyone?

No treatment for Crohn's disease works for everyone, and this is no exception. This type of therapy works particularly well in people with small-bowel Crohn's disease. It works much less often in patients with Crohn's disease of the colon.

Tube Feeding

There are three situations in which liquid diets are taken by tube. They are:

- when a patient cannot drink enough to achieve an energy goal because he or she cannot find a product that is palatable;
- to reduce or prevent side effects such as nausea or diarrhea;
- to administer a product which is *meant* to be given by tube, usually because it is simply undrinkable because of its taste or some other feature.

The tube is inserted into the stomach through the nose. This sounds unpleasant, but the tubes are small and soft, and generally they are well tolerated. Although the liquid diet can be dripped in through the tube using gravity alone, it is often administered using a pump. For some people, controlling the rate of delivery with the pump is important; for others it is not. Battery-operated pumps allow people to move around both in and out of hospital during the process.

Some adults will do almost anything to avoid being tube-fed. Children, on the other hand, adapt well to this form of treatment (see Chapter 8).

Advantages of Liquid-Diet Therapy
If nutritional therapy is to be used, one of the greatest advantages of a liquid diet is that the majority of people can stay out of hospital while using it. It is also a safe means of treatment, provided the doctor or dietitian instructing you is familiar with it. You do not have to stay home. You can go to work, school, or anywhere else. As long as you are able to consume the desired amount of energy per day, you really have no restrictions whatsoever on your activities.

Disadvantages of Liquid-Diet Therapy
Nevertheless, liquid-diet therapy has several disadvantages. One is cost. Of course, when you are not eating a regular diet, that cost saving must be taken into account. But generally it does not cancel out the cost of the specialized diet. Unfortunately, insurance companies rarely pay for these products, claiming they are food and not treatment. Some government health plans do pay, but for specific groups only.

A second disadvantage is taste fatigue. Many people find they can take these products for a few days but get bored with the taste after that. Even when people can handle these products for longer, most prefer one flavor. This again leads to taste fatigue. Using a variety of clear fluids, flavorings, or recipes helps. Water-based products, for example, can be made into a slush or even frozen.

Ultimately you will have to stop the liquid-diet therapy. Even if you feel perfectly well on a liquid diet, only after you stop the diet will you and your doctor know if anything has really been accomplished. As soon as you go back on regular food, your previous symptoms of Crohn's disease may immediately reappear.

Additional problems for some people on liquid diets include nausea, a perpetual feeling of unpleasant fullness, abdominal cramps, and frequent or loose stools. Obviously some of these side effects can easily be confused with the Crohn's disease that is being treated. You can reduce these side effects by sipping the product *slowly*; take 30 to 60 minutes for one can or box, especially during the first few days. Although some people have one small bowel movement every few days, one to three loose movements a day should not be considered a problem.

Can You Have Any Regular Food While on a Liquid Diet?
Most of these products do not provide enough water. I tell my patients to take the liquid diet when hungry and clear fluids when thirsty. You can also have clear fluids to combat taste fatigue, provided that you still achieve your daily energy goal.

How Long Should You Stay on a Liquid Diet?
There are no rules about how long to stay on a liquid diet and a lot depends on your physician's experience. I tell my patients that they have to fulfill two conditions before they can go back to regular food. First, they have to take the liquid diet for a minimum of two weeks. Second, they must feel perfectly well for a minimum of one week. If a patient feels much better but not perfectly well and has not improved further for a week, then I compromise and accept partial improvement. Generally, the maximum period I prescribe a liquid diet for is eight weeks.

TPN – Total Parenteral Nutrition
In the term "total parenteral nutrition" or TPN, "total" refers to providing a nutritionally complete diet; "parenteral" means that the diet is given by a route other than the GI tract. In the

late 1960s, it became possible to feed people high-energy diets intravenously. This meant that people with Crohn's disease could avoid food, improve, and still receive adequate nutrition. In the 1970s this was a popular treatment for the disease. However, in the late 1970s and through the early 1980s it became increasingly obvious that most such people could be equally well treated with oral liquid diets. As awareness of the risks and expense of TPN grew, more and more patients were treated with liquid diets. For some, nutritional therapy was a combination of a liquid diet and parenteral nutrition (PPN, or *partial* PN).

Today, TPN and PPN are reserved mainly for patients who are acutely ill, such as those with severe colitis or toxic mega-colon (see Chapter 9). Many of these people can't or won't eat enough to maintain adequate nutrition.

Occasionally people with Crohn's disease need prolonged temporary or even permanent PN to maintain adequate nutrition. Others require a long period of nutritional build-up prior to surgery and cannot take in food through the GI tract. Still others – fortunately not very many – have had most of their small bowel removed surgically and don't have enough intestine left to absorb all nutrients (short-bowel syndrome). Such people receive HPN, or home parenteral nutrition. Just as with home tube feeding, those on HPN become quite knowledge-able and self-reliant about administering the IV diet and maintaining the IV site. Some hospitals have HPN programs to teach the technique.

The main advantages of TPN at the present time are that it can prevent or reduce nutritional deterioration in seriously ill patients, and it can be a virtual lifeline to people unable to get proper nutrition because of an inadequate amount of intestine.

The main disadvantages are that TPN is highly specialized and expensive. Furthermore, the need to have foreign material (the IV line) in the body constantly puts the person at risk of blood infections and blood clots – both potentially life-threatening complications. Another risk is the possible development of liver inflammation; this can lead to cirrhosis of the liver, which in turn may cause liver failure.

High-Glutamine Products

Glutamine is a nonessential amino acid. "Nonessential" means that the body is able to produce it, in comparison with "essential" amino acids, which must be taken in because the body is unable to manufacture them. During physical stresses such as surgery or severe illness, the body may need more glutamine than it can produce.

Research has shown that glutamine is an important nutrient for the jejunum. This has led some manufacturers of nutritional support products to promote high-glutamine products. But there is little evidence that glutamine is beneficial to the ileum, where the majority of small-bowel Crohn's disease occurs, and there is no conclusive evidence that high-glutamine products offer any special benefit to people with Crohn's disease generally.

Some Unnecessary Dietary Restrictions in IBD

Some people need to restrict their diet all the time, others need to do it some of the time, and some can always eat a perfectly normal diet.

Many people, however, restrict their diets unnecessarily. Sometimes the doctor has imposed these restrictions, but in other cases they are self-imposed.

For example, many people avoid foods they can recognize in their bowel movements because of the mistaken belief that there is something wrong with their digestion. Humans cannot digest (break down) many of the components of dietary fiber. If you eat corn, you will see corn in your stool. The same is true for a large variety of skins, seeds, and other fibrous foods. This is normal.

Is It Necessary to Avoid Fried or Spicy Foods?

For the vast majority of people with IBD, there is absolutely no need to avoid fried or spicy foods. Many such people are underweight, particularly when they have been ill, and fat is an excellent source of energy. Fried foods not only taste good, but help you regain lost weight. Spices improve taste, which helps to increase food intake.

I am not suggesting you eat a high-fat diet, since fat may increase the risk of heart disease and other diseases in some people. But when you're trying to regain weight, it is generally harmless to eat an increased amount of fat. When I have a patient who is having trouble gaining weight after a flare-up of IBD, I often suggest high-fat, high-energy foods such as bacon and eggs, potato chips, and various fried foods.

Adverse Effects of Unnecessary Restrictions

If you avoid two or three foods because you think they may increase your symptoms, it's generally not a problem. But if you have a long list of foods that you avoid, it's likely that your disease is active and needs specific therapy. Avoiding a large number of foods usually decreases your appetite, because your diet becomes boring. Eating less, of course, reduces the amount of energy you take in, which leads to weight loss. Someone with active disease is likely already underweight, and losing more weight is undesirable.

Three Steps to Avoiding Self-imposed Dietary Restrictions

- Avoid restrictions based on hearsay. When I ask patients why they are avoiding certain foods, they sometimes tell me that they "heard somewhere" that such a food "could" cause symptoms. Friends are rarely a reliable source of medical or nutritional advice. Relatives can be even worse, because they *care* about you.

- If you think you've found a relationship between certain foods and certain symptoms, discuss your theory with your physician before you limit yourself permanently.

- If you're older, especially if you live alone, put more effort into preparing meals. Otherwise your diet will be boring, you'll eat less, and you'll lose weight. Older people, especially when they are ill, need balanced meals.

Remember, dietary restrictions should be discussed with your doctor or a registered dietitian. You can experiment yourself, but do not maintain any long-term restrictions without letting your doctor know.

SIX

Drugs and IBD

Before getting into the details of drug therapy, I must remind you of the old saying "A little learning is a dangerous thing." Knowledge is good, but it must be in context. Some people see the side effects of medications (or other treatments) and say, "Wow, look at the risks! I'm not going to do that!" But *not* doing something may also have risks. Not taking a treatment may mean that the illness will get worse or more complicated. The potential benefits and risks of any decision should be carefully considered by you and your doctor.

It's also important to be aware that there are "generic" side effects that have nothing to do with particular medications. For example, many tablets contain lactose, and some people have such extreme lactose intolerance (see Chapter 5) that this will affect them. Some tablets are large and difficult to swallow. A variety of medications used in IBD are taken in the form of an enema; there is a small but real risk of puncturing the rectum with the plastic enema tip.

...ed to treat IBD can be divided into two categories.
...ncludes those that reduce inflammation; this in turn
... symptoms such as diarrhea and pain. The second
... ...les those that have no effect on inflammation but may
be useful in reducing or eliminating symptoms, especially diarrhea and crampy pain. In both categories, not all side effects are discussed, due to space limitations. Of course, in addition to drugs there are several nondrug therapies, such as dietary changes, covered in Chapter 5, and surgery, which we'll cover in Chapter 7.

Drugs That Reduce Inflammation

Sulfasalazine

In the late 1930s, Dr. Nana Svartz, a Swedish researcher, proposed linking one of the newly discovered sulfa drugs with acetylsalicylic acid (ASA) to treat the painful joint disease rheumatoid arthritis, at that time thought to be caused by an infection. The first patient Dr. Svartz treated with such a combined drug, called sulfasalazine, happened to have ulcerative colitis as well. The most striking benefit for this patient was control of his colitis. Until the introduction of sulfasalazine in 1942, no medication had been able to control colitis. For the next eight years it remained the *only* drug available for the treatment of colitis, until 1950, when cortisone was introduced. Sulfasalazine continued to be the only drug in its class until the 1980s, when pure 5-ASA (5-aminosalicylate, the active ingredient of sulfasalazine) became available.

Many gastroenterologists now prefer to prescribe the newer 5-ASA drugs, but some still start with sulfasalazine. It's just as effective, it's cheaper, and it's familiar. The only drawback compared with pure 5-ASA is that sulfasalazine more often has side effects.

How Does It Work?

The 5-aminosalicylate (5-ASA) portion of the sulfasalazine, the active ingredient, limits the production of certain chemical products of inflammation that promote diarrhea. It also removes oxygen radicals from tissues. These substances, released during inflammation, are toxic to cells. Like all sulfa drugs, sulfasalazine is an antibacterial agent. This means that it prevents some bacteria from functioning and causing illness, although it does not kill them. At the present time, the antibacterial activity is not thought to be important in ulcerative colitis. It may have some value in Crohn's disease, but there is not much evidence for this, even though antibiotics – which *kill* bacteria – are clearly beneficial.

When Is It Used?

Sulfasalazine can be used to treat mild to moderate attacks of ulcerative colitis and Crohn's disease. But it is most valuable because it markedly *reduces the chance* of a flare-up of ulcerative colitis in most patients. If taken regularly, it continues to have this effect indefinitely. This does not guarantee you will not have a flare-up, but for most people it significantly lessens the risk. A similar effect has not been proven in Crohn's disease, but some people appear to do well on the drug. Sulfasalazine has not been shown to reduce the risk of Crohn's disease coming back after surgery. It is also used to treat arthritis, which occurs in about 20 percent of people with IBD.

What Are the Side Effects?

The most frequent side effects of sulfasalazine are gastrointestinal. Nausea and reduced appetite are common, but of course these can also be symptoms of IBD. Vomiting is less common. These side effects can sometimes be prevented if you start with a small dose of the drug and build it up slowly, rather than starting with a full dose on the first day. It also helps to take the pills with food and not on an empty stomach. A coated form of sulfasalazine releases the drug more slowly, and is particularly helpful in reducing any nausea due to the drug.

The second most common type of side effect is an allergic reaction. This usually appears as an itchy rash (hives) or swelling of the hands and/or some or all of the face. In someone who has never taken the drug before, the reaction generally occurs 14 to 21 days after starting the drug. In someone who has taken the drug before, it generally occurs within the first week. Report any allergic reactions to your doctor immediately. About 70 percent of the people who have an allergic reaction to this drug can be desensitized, so that the drug can be gradually reintroduced. Occasionally allergic reactions will be associated with arthritis (inflamed joints), hepatitis (inflamed liver), fever, or many other inflammations of tissues and organs. *Desensitization should not be attempted in such cases.*

The third type of common side effect involves the blood. Red blood cells normally have a life span of 120 days. These blood cells are then taken up by the spleen, destroyed, and replaced by new red blood cells from the bone marrow, in a normal process that goes on all the time. In some people, sulfasalazine causes the red blood cells to be destroyed prematurely. This process is called hemolysis, from "heme," meaning blood, and "lysis," meaning breakdown. Hemolysis is generally reversible and can be controlled in some patients simply by reducing the dose of sulfasalazine; in others, the drug must be stopped completely.

Folic acid (also known as folate) is one of the B vitamins, and one of the building blocks of red blood cells. Another blood-related side effect of sulfasalazine is that it can reduce the ability of the intestine to absorb folic acid, possibly leading to anemia. Physicians will prescribe a daily folic acid pill when necessary.

A rare but serious side effect of sulfasalazine is bone-marrow shutdown (marrow aplasia). In addition to red blood cells, the bone marrow makes white blood cells and platelets. With this side effect, the production of any or all types of blood cells may stop. Treatments for this exist but are not always effective, and death can result. Bone-marrow shutdown usually occurs within the first three months of therapy, but it also represents the most serious long-term risk of sulfasalazine. Unusual bleeding or bruising should be reported immediately to your doctor.

Occasionally sulfasalazine can reduce a man's sperm count enough to make him infertile. Stopping the drug allows the count to return to normal, though this may take up to three months.

Headaches can also occur with sulfasalazine. In some people they are mild, but in others they are severe enough that the drug must be stopped. Many patients who take sulfasalazine notice that their urine is orange-yellow. Yellowing of the skin and soft contact lenses has occasionally been reported, but this discoloration is harmless.

Sulfasalazine comes in tablets, either coated or uncoated; in a liquid form (suspension) that is orange-lemon in flavor and odor; and, in some countries, as an enema or suppository.

5-Aminosalicylate (5-ASA)

The active ingredient in sulfasalazine, 5-ASA, does not have any antibacterial properties. Although it is chemically similar

---

Because brands of drugs come and go, I have used generic ("no-name") drug names. For the brand names available in early 2003, see the drug table at the end of the book.

to ASA, 5-ASA doesn't do anything that ASA does, and ASA doesn't do anything that 5-ASA does. This drug was introduced in the 1980s and is now widely used.

How Does It Work?

Like sulfasalazine, 5-ASA reduces the production of certain chemicals in the intestine that cause diarrhea. It also inactivates oxygen radicals that destroy tissue.

When Is It Used?

5-ASA can be used to treat mild to moderate attacks of ulcerative colitis and Crohn's disease. For people with proctitis or colitis limited to the last one to two feet (30 to 60 centimeters) of the colon, small doses taken rectally are frequently more effective than much larger doses taken orally. The drug is also used to reduce the chance of flare-ups of both these diseases in many people. Used postoperatively, 5-ASA has been shown to reduce the risk of recurrent small-bowel Crohn's disease, although the reduction is modest, and more apparent in women than in men.

What Are the Side Effects?

Many of the side effects of 5-ASA are similar to those of sulfasalazine. But they occur much less commonly, because the sulfa portion of sulfasalazine responsible for many of those adverse effects is absent in 5-ASA.

Common side effects include nausea and headaches. Diarrhea occurs occasionally — more with one form of the drug, olsalazine, than with others. The diarrhea may be reduced by introducing the drug gradually and taking it with food.

Other less common side effects include allergic reactions (e.g., itchy rash and swelling of the hands and face, and/or fever). As with sulfasalazine, some allergic patients can be desensitized. A severe, dull, steady pain across the upper abdomen, sometimes with back pain, may indicate pancreatitis (inflammation of the pancreas). If pancreatitis occurs, 5-ASA cannot be used again.

In rare cases, an attack of ulcerative colitis, or a worsening of an attack, will occur with 5-ASA. The drug must be stopped and the attack treated in some other way.

Hair loss has occasionally been reported as a side effect, but the reliability of the reports is questionable. There is a normal process of hair turnover, in which a certain number of hairs fall out every day and are replaced by new ones. It is extremely common for this turnover to be accelerated during an illness, and especially in the weeks afterwards. You may notice more hair in your comb or brush, and more hair in the shower or bathtub. If you have long hair, you are much more likely to be aware of this. But the loss is temporary; new hair is growing in. Hair loss is serious only if the hair comes out in clumps and leaves bald patches. This type of hair loss has been reported with 5-ASA only very rarely.

Patients commonly use 5-ASA enemas or suppositories as maintenance therapy. The chronic use of any sort of enema or suppository can irritate the anal canal and produce pain and bleeding.

Research has suggested that kidney damage *may* be a side effect of long-term use of this drug. It is not unusual for patients on 5-ASA to have an excessive number of white blood cells in the urine. Having your urine and kidney function checked periodically (e.g., once yearly) when you use 5-ASA is recommended.

5-ASA is available in tablets, enemas, and suppositories. A rectal foam is on the market in some countries, but not yet in North America.

There are several brands of 5-ASA tablets available at the present time. Each brand "targets" the 5-ASA to specific sites

---

Common Questions about 5-ASA

Q: Is one 5-ASA product better than any other for the treatment of small-bowel Crohn's disease?

A: The 5-ASA products that target the small bowel and colon are all approximately equal; the minor differences in formulation have not been studied comparatively.

Q: Is there any evidence that a person with colitis should be treated with a 5-ASA product that is targeted specifically at the colon?

A: While there are some published data suggesting that this is the case, the evidence is not compelling. It appears that all the oral forms are effective in colitis.

Q: Is there any point in trying 5-ASA enemas or suppositories if oral 5-ASA does not appear to be working?

A: Definitely yes! Rectally administered 5-ASA is often effective (even in very small doses) when oral 5-ASA is not (even in maximum doses).

Q: If I am doing well on sulfasalazine, should I switch to a "pure" 5-ASA product?

A: Most gastroenterologists agree that you should not "rock the boat." There is a somewhat greater risk of diarrhea as a side effect with 5-ASA; this is unpredictable and occasionally severe.

Q: If my ulcerative colitis has been inactive for several years, should I stop my sulfasalazine or 5-ASA medication?

A: Not without asking your doctor. The main function of these medications is to reduce the risk of a flare-up.

---

in the intestine. Whether these differences are of clinical significance has not yet been demonstrated. In addition to 5-ASA, other generic names for these products include mesalamine, mesalazine, and olsalazine. The newest product in this group is balsalazide, which consists of a unit of 5-ASA linked to an inert carrier. One recent study suggests that balsalazide may be a little more effective than the pure 5-ASA products, but more studies are needed.

Steroids

The steroids used in IBD, known as glucocorticosteroids or glucocorticoids, are derivatives of cortisol, a natural steroid produced by the adrenal glands, which sit on top of the kidneys.

Glucocorticoids are different from the anabolic steroids used by some athletes to enhance performance, and also used by doctors to treat certain diseases. The first glucocorticoid to be given to patients was cortisone, in 1950. The introduction of this potent drug revolutionized the treatment of many chronic diseases, including IBD. Currently the most-used glucocorticoids are prednisone and prednisolone.

How Do These Steroids Work?
Quite simply, glucocorticoids reduce inflammation.

When Are They Used?
These drugs are used to treat most moderate and severe attacks of ulcerative colitis and Crohn's disease. In people with ulcerative colitis, once the attack has settled down significantly, the dose should gradually be reduced to zero over several weeks. There is no evidence that steroids prevent flare-ups of ulcerative colitis, so people with this disease should generally not remain on this medication between attacks. About 5 percent of those with ulcerative colitis have what is referred to as "chronic continuous colitis." With these people it may not be possible to get the dosage down to zero between attacks. Many of them require continuous steroid therapy to stay well.

It is much more common for people to require continuous steroid therapy in Crohn's disease, to suppress chronic symptoms not controllable by other measures. However, many people with Crohn's disease require steroids only intermittently. Still others do not need them at all. Steroids do not prevent Crohn's disease from recurring after surgery.

When either ulcerative colitis or Crohn's colitis is limited to the last one to two feet (30 to 60 centimeters) of the colon, glucocorticoids may be just as effective rectally as similar or larger doses taken orally, with fewer side effects.

What Are the Side Effects?
Steroids have both visible and invisible side effects.

Visible side effects: The visible side effects are more upsetting to you than to your doctor. It's not that your doctor doesn't care, but he or she knows that these effects are reversible weeks to months after the drug has been stopped. Also, these side effects are not dangerous in themselves. They include:

- rounding of the face – appears gradually;
- redness of the face, usually mild – creates a "healthier" appearance;
- increased appetite and weight gain, usually desirable;
- mood changes – often happier because of feeling better; feeling nervous or jittery; serious extremes of mood such as euphoria or severe depression are very uncommon;
- acne – mild to severe; may require antibiotics; mostly in individuals taking steroids for weeks or more; usually improves with dose reduction, but occasionally first appears, or becomes much worse, shortly after steroids stopped;
- increased energy and insomnia – some people sleep fewer hours and yet do not get sleepy during the day; you may need a sleeping pill temporarily, particularly with big doses;
- ankle swelling, in malnourished people;
- weakness of the muscles of the thighs and upper arms – difficulty climbing stairs and getting up from a seat without using your arms;
- night sweats – may also be a sign of illness;
- facial hair growth – rarely noticeable;
- skinny arms and a pot belly – with long-term therapy (years);

- a hump of fat on the middle of the upper back – with long-term therapy (years);
- easy bruising and thinning of the skin; mainly with long-term therapy;
- reduced growth rate and delayed puberty;
- muscle and joint stiffness soon after a course of oral steroids is completed.

Invisible side effects: These are of greater concern to your doctor, because they can cause irreversible harm. They include:

- softening of the bones – especially hips and spine; mainly with long-term therapy (years) but occasionally with short-term (weeks); physical inactivity, malnutrition, and a low-lactose diet increase risk, which can now be monitored with bone densitometry (also known as bone density testing);
- reduced immunity – increased risk of infections; mainly with high doses and hospitalized patients;

Important Points to Remember about Glucocorticoid Steroid Therapy

- Never stop steroids suddenly, unless clearly advised to do so by your doctor. The usual practice is to taper the dose until it is down to zero, although if steroids have been taken for two weeks or less they can be stopped abruptly, if this is desired.
- Always advise any physician, dentist, or paramedical person treating you that you are or have been on steroids within the previous twelve months. Some physicians recommend that you wear a medical-alert bracelet if you're on steroids.
- Remind your own physician that you have been on steroids within the previous twelve months if you are being treated for an acute illness. Your doctor must keep track of hundreds of patients; you have only one – you!

- aggravation of diabetes mellitus– increased blood sugar, usually temporary;
- cataracts – mainly with higher doses and prolonged therapy;
- increased eye pressure (glaucoma) – more common in children;
- reduced potassium level, also a result of diarrhea; can contribute to weakness;
- high blood pressure – very uncommon;
- ulcers of the stomach and/or duodenum (controversial); only with high doses, if at all.

Stopping Steroids

The last invisible side effect may occur days to months after you stop taking steroids. Your body normally makes cortisol in the adrenal glands. When it is subjected to physical stress (e.g., fever, surgery, etc.), it produces up to ten times more cortisol. With *extreme* psychological stress, there can be a very temporary increase in cortisol. When you take a glucocorticoid, normal cortisol production decreases or stops completely. When you stop taking the steroid, production begins again, but may be sluggish for up to a year. This means that you may need extra steroids at a time of physical stress, for up to twelve months after you have come off the medication. The extra steroids may be necessary for days or longer, depending on the illness. If the stress is mental, the dose should be increased for only one to two days, *if at all*. Symptoms of insufficient cortisol are nonspecific. They include nausea, extreme fatigue, weakness, light-headedness, and possibly diarrhea. If you suspect that you are not producing enough cortisol soon after stopping steroids, *discuss it with your doctor.*

Forms of Steroids

There are many different forms of cortisonelike steroids. They are available as tablets (e.g., prednisone), suppositories (e.g., hydrocortisone), enemas (e.g., budesonide), rectal foams (hydrocortisone), and injectable forms (e.g., hydrocortisone, methylprednisolone, ACTH).

Budesonide is a newer steroid, available as oral capsules and as an enema. It has fewer short-term side effects; this is thought to be because it acts locally, at the site of disease in the intestine. When budesonide is absorbed into the bloodstream, it is metabolized (broken down) more rapidly into inactive components. With long-term use of budesonide the kinds of side effects listed above may appear, though there is some evidence that osteoporosis may be less of a problem.

Other Points about Steroids

If you need long-term steroid therapy, your doctor may tell you to try taking a double dose every second day and skipping the days in between – so-called alternate-day dosing. It is supposed to be just as effective, with fewer net side effects. However, many people complain that they simply do not feel as well on the "off" days, so this is not widely used.

People being treated with rectal steroids can often retain suppositories or foam much more easily than liquid enemas, sometimes with equal benefit.

Immunosuppressive (Immunomodulator) Drugs

Immunosuppressives are another class of drugs used in the treatment of IBD. They were originally introduced to treat certain cancers. They have also been used to help prevent rejection in organ transplants. In both these situations, relatively large doses of the drugs are administered. It has been known for more than 45 years, however, that smaller doses of immunosuppressives can be used effectively to treat a variety of other conditions, including IBD. The most exciting recent development with this class of drugs has been the demonstration that some of them can heal Crohn's disease. But remember, healing is not curing. If something is cured, treatment can be stopped. To maintain healing, treatment must continue.

How Do They Work?

So far, all the drugs in this class work by suppressing Th1 production; this allows Th2 production to increase. (See Chapter 2, regarding "rebalancing" immune functions.) Studies are underway with treatments that actually *stimulate* Th2 production. This is exciting, because we hope that by avoiding suppression of the immune system we can reduce the side effects generally associated with immunosuppressives. In the future, the term "immunomodulator" (meaning "modifying immune function") will probably replace the term "immunosuppressive," reflecting the expansion of this class of drugs.

When Are They Used?

These drugs are most often used when there is a desire to reduce, eliminate, or avoid the use of steroids. Both ulcerative colitis patients and Crohn's disease patients who need frequent or continuous steroid therapy can often reduce their dosage, or even stop steroids altogether, if they take these drugs.

In ulcerative colitis, immunosuppressive drugs usually work within two to twelve weeks, if there is going to be a response. Because some of these drugs act slowly in Crohn's disease, you may have to wait up to six months or more for a benefit, though some people respond more quickly. Because the drugs act so slowly, it is often necessary to increase steroids temporarily.

Here is a typical case. A 27-year-old man with Crohn's disease sought a second opinion because he could not stop taking steroids. He had a history of extensive surgery, so another operation was undesirable. Despite steroids, he was having daily crampy pain and diarrhea. He was put on 6-mercaptopurine (6-MP). One month later, he was told to try to reduce the prednisone. He promptly began to have more symptoms of Crohn's disease, and had to increase his prednisone again. One month later, he again reduced his prednisone, with the same result. The next month all of his Crohn's symptoms gradually disappeared. He was able to reduce his prednisone until he was off steroids. He continued on the 6-MP alone and remained well.

What Are the Side Effects?

The most worrisome side effect of all immunosuppressive drugs is that they reduce the effectiveness of your immune system, though this is not common with the doses used for IBD. Resistance to infections decreases, which can be serious in the case of unusual infections that may be difficult to diagnose and treat. You should report any fever, chills, or persistent sore throat to your doctor promptly.

Larger doses of immunosuppressives – such as those used in transplant patients and people being treated for certain types of cancer – increase the risk of malignancy, particularly the kind known as lymphoma. Several recent studies state that there is no increased risk with the lower doses used in IBD, but some researchers think there may be a very slightly higher risk than in the general population.

The Main Immunosuppressive Drugs

Azathioprine and 6-mercaptopurine:
- used in IBD for more than 45 years;
- the best long-term strategy for many people with IBD;
- azathioprine is converted to 6-mercaptopurine (6-MP) in the body;
- equally effective;
- can heal (not cure) Crohn's disease in some people;
- some side effects (nausea, rash) with one may not occur with the other;
- lowering of blood cell counts is reversible but occasionally life-threatening;
- lowering of white blood cell count is enhanced by all 5-ASA drugs;
- pancreatitis can occur weeks or months after starting therapy;
- convenient once-a-day dose;
- 6-thioguanine (6-TG), produced from 6-MP, may have less effect on blood cell counts; there have been no controlled trials, and long-term side effects are a concern.

Methotrexate
- available for fifty years, but first used in IBD in late 1980s;
- often given by injection, but well absorbed and effective as tablets taken by mouth;
- once-weekly dosing is attractive;
- a good alternative to azathioprine or 6-mercaptopurine for both forms of IBD;
- benefit is expected within two to twelve weeks of starting therapy;

- common side effects are nausea and mouth ulcers, reduced by folate supplementation;
- can cause cirrhosis of the liver with long-term use; extent of risk unknown.

Cyclosporine (Cyclosporin A)
- first used in IBD in late 1980s;
- potentially severe side effects, including kidney damage, high blood pressure, liver damage;
- also causes increased facial hair and enlargement of the gums;
- risk of side effects is reduced by monitoring blood levels of drug;
- low-dose cyclosporine does not prevent flare-ups of Crohn's;
- reduces urgent need for surgery in severe ulcerative colitis but many people need surgery within six to twelve months;
- usually replaced by azathioprine or 6-mercaptopurine if attack subsides;
- available as capsules, or oral or intravenous solution.

Tacrolimus (also known as FK506)
- an antibiotic with immunosuppressive properties;
- first used as an anti-rejection drug in transplantation;
- studied for IBD since 1995;
- a potential alternative to cyclosporine;
- common side effects include tremor, elevated blood sugar, high blood pressure, kidney damage and infection, none considered severe in early reports;
- needs more study.

Mycophenolate Mofetil
- another relatively new immunosuppressive;
- first used as an anti-rejection drug in transplantation;
- studied for IBD since 1998;
- common side effects include nausea;
- can cause a drug-induced colitis;
- needs more study in small-bowel Crohn's; probably should not be used in colitis;

Thalidomide
- old drug with a new use;
- has anti-TNF activity (see "Infliximab," below);
- first used for ulcerative colitis in 1979;
- studied in both ulcerative colitis and Crohn's disease since 1997;
- common side effects include mild drowsiness, dry mouth, dry skin, and tingling, burning, numbness, or pain in the hands, arms, feet, or legs;
- needs more study.

Biologicals

The term "biologicals" has been coined to describe a powerful new class of drugs that have arisen as a result of the science of molecular biology, and our ability to use this science to develop new therapies. The main characteristic of these agents is that they target specific molecules involved in the inflammatory process.

Infliximab
This is the first of the biologicals. Infliximab is a murine, chimeric, monoclonal antibody directed toward tumor necrosis factor-alpha (TNF-alpha). "Murine" means that it's produced in mice; "chimeric" means that its chemistry is a blend

of two different species – it's about 75 percent human protein, and 25 percent mouse protein. Because it's directed at TNF-alpha, it is often referred to as an anti-TNF drug.

Don't be alarmed! This treatment has nothing to do with tumors; the name relates to the way TNF was discovered. The word "necrosis" means cell damage, but this treatment does not damage cells. Infliximab is given by intravenous infusion. People with fistulas are given an initial course of three infusions; the second is two weeks after the first, and the third is four weeks after that. The initial treatment for people without fistulas is a single infusion.

Two of the great benefits of this drug are that it works within two weeks and that it can heal (not cure) Crohn's disease.

How does it work?
TNF is a major promoter of inflammation. It also has an important function in keeping certain dormant diseases in check. In simple terms, infliximab works by blocking the effects of TNF. Many of the details of how this is achieved are still to be worked out. The duration of the benefit is quite variable, but averages eight to twelve weeks. People notice the effect wearing off, and request a repeat infusion.

When is it used?
At the time of writing, the main reason to use this medication in IBD is for people with moderate or severe Crohn's disease that is unresponsive or poorly responsive to other conventional therapies. Infliximab can be particularly helpful for people with complex fistulas but, like every treatment for Crohn's disease, it only works in some people. It seems to be more likely to work in nonsmokers and people who are also on immunosuppressives.

To date, infliximab has been used in a small number of people with ulcerative colitis; controlled studies are underway to determine whether it works in that disease. It has also been used to treat some of the other manifestations of IBD, such as ankylosing spondylitis and pyoderma gangrenosum.

So far, the only other common disease being treated with this drug is rheumatoid arthritis. People with IBD can have this disease as well, but the frequency is the same as for the general population.

What are the side effects?

In Crohn's disease studies, about 5 percent of patients had to stop receiving the drug because of side effects. The main reasons were infusion reactions or subsequent infections. Typical reactions include headache, nausea, light-headedness, flushing and hives. A few people develop chest pain or shortness of breath. Infusion reactions are fairly common, occurring in about 15 percent of people, but most are mild and do not require the drug to be withdrawn. In less than 1 percent of cases does the infusion have to be stopped and not restarted; usually it can be restarted at a slower rate, or after administration of a medication such as an antihistamine, or acetaminophen for headache.

It appears that people who are frequently exposed to mice (such as lab technicians) are more likely to have a significant reaction. A markedly longer than usual interval (more than twenty weeks) between infusions may be associated with a greater chance of a reaction in adults, but not in children; this needs further study.

Another side effect is an increased risk of infection. Some of these infections are serious. Many people carry dormant tuberculosis (TB) bacteria, and an important beneficial function of TNF is preventing the TB from becoming active. In some people, when the TNF is blocked, active TB infection occurs. This seems to happen mostly to people who are on immunosuppressive medication. This has led the maker of infliximab to recommend that anyone who is going to be treated first have a TB skin test, and a chest X-ray. If there is evidence of TB, it must be treated first, or infliximab should not be given. Some other, more unusual infections may also occur as a result of infliximab therapy.

Some people treated with infliximab develop anti-nuclear antibodies (ANA, also known as ANF, for "anti-nuclear factor"). These antibodies are frequently present in people with the disease known as lupus (systemic lupus erythematosus, or SLE). Some people (with or without IBD) test positive for lupus without having the disease. A few people who were treated with infliximab and who had a positive ANA test later developed lupus, which required treatment with steroids. (The treatment was successful.) Several drugs used to treat other conditions are also known to cause lupus or a lupus-like condition.

In early studies, infliximab appeared to increase the risk of lymphoma (lymph gland cancer); in later studies, the occurrence of this condition was less frequent. At the time of writing, it is unknown whether this is a true side effect.

As this is still a new drug (the first clinical report came in 1995), it will be some time before we are knowledgeable about the long-term safety of infliximab.

CDP-571

- not yet on the market;
- a "humanized" anti-TNF antibody, meaning that there is less non-human protein content than in infliximab;
- may cause fewer immunological side effects compared to infliximab;
- so far, not as good as infliximab.

Etanercept

- another anti-TNF antibody;
- 100 percent human;
- side effects a concern;
- now used in rheumatoid arthritis;
- studies in Crohn's have been disappointing.

Natalizumab

Substances called cellular adhesion molecules (CAMs) regulate the entry of white blood cells into normal and inflamed segments of the intestine. CAMs cause certain white cells to adhere to the inner surfaces of blood vessels; once they are stuck there, they are able to move through the vessel wall and into the tissues of the gut wall, causing the inflammatory process. Some CAMs, such as alpha4 integrin, are located on the surface of white blood cells, while others are on the surface of the blood vessels. In IBD, most of these CAMs are overactive. Recently, compounds have been designed to work against the CAMs; these are the latest biologicals being tested in IBD. Natalizumab is an anti-alpha4 integrin antibody.

How does it work?

Natalizumab acts by preventing lymphocytes (a type of white blood cell) from sticking to the inner lining cells of the blood vessels. If they don't stick, they won't enter the surrounding tissues.

When is it used?

Like infliximab, natalizumab is given intravenously. At the time of writing, this drug is not yet on the market; how much to give, and how often, are still being worked out.

What are the side effects?
Side effects so far have been few, but studies are ongoing. We may expect an increased risk of infections, since white blood cells are needed outside the blood vessels to fight infections.

Other Biologicals

Another anti-alpha4 integrin, known as LDP-02, has been designed, but testing is not as far advanced as with natalizumab. It is currently being tested in both ulcerative colitis and Crohn's disease. Several clinical studies have been reported with alicaforsen (ISIS-2302), an anti-ICAM (intercellular adhesion molecule), also known as an "antisense oligonucleotide," in people with Crohn's disease who are resistant to steroids. So far, results with this agent have been disappointing. Studies with recombinant human interleukin-10 and interleukin-11 (rhuIL-10, rhuIL-11) are ongoing.

Granulocyte-monocyte colony-stimulating factor (GM-CSF), which enhances white blood cell function, produced impressive results in a handful of people with Crohn's.

Growth hormone injections improved some Crohn's patients, but the study was brief.

Antibiotics

Over the years, a variety of antibiotics have been used in the treatment of both ulcerative colitis and Crohn's disease. Antibiotics are not a primary therapy for ulcerative colitis, but may be given along with other forms of therapy. However, they may be used as a primary therapy in Crohn's disease, with no other medication or treatment given.

Antibiotics in Ulcerative Colitis

Antibiotics used in ulcerative colitis are generally classified as "broad spectrum." This means they are effective against a large number of different bacteria. Commonly used antibiotics in this group are ampicillin, cefazolin, gentamicin, tobramycin, ciprofloxacin, and metronidazole. Numerous other broad-spectrum antibiotics are less commonly used, mainly because they are more expensive, without added benefits.

Some gastroenterologists rarely use antibiotics in treating people with ulcerative colitis. But doctors who do prescribe them usually use them for severe attacks. When the colon is badly inflamed, the bacteria normally present can easily penetrate the intestinal wall and move into the surrounding tissues, even the bloodstream. This can produce serious complications. Two of the most serious are septicemia (infected blood) and one or more abscesses (boils) in the liver.

Metronidazole in Crohn's Disease

The antibiotic used the most in Crohn's disease is metronidazole. It is particularly effective against a group of intestinal bacteria known as anaerobes – bacteria that do best in tissues where there is little or no oxygen.

In Crohn's disease, the full thickness of the intestinal wall is inflamed. Little breaks can develop in the inner lining of the intestine, and these breaks can lead to little openings, called sinus tracts, that penetrate through the wall of the bowel into the surrounding tissues. These sinus tracts frequently result in abscesses, and sometimes fistulas as well (see Chapter 9). Metronidazole is particularly useful in the treatment of abscesses (boils) and fistulas at or near the anus. It is available as capsules or tablets, or in injectable form.

Metronidazole has been shown to benefit some people with Crohn's colitis. Someone who has not responded to sulfasalazine may respond to metronidazole; however, someone who has not responded to metronidazole is unlikely to respond

Metronidazole and Alcohol

It was previously thought that anyone on metronidazole should avoid alcohol totally, but further experience has shown that not everyone reacts to this combination.

If you wish to drink, experiment first with very small amounts. If you want to drink beer, try just a mouthful, then two mouthfuls on another occasion, and so on. If you get to half a cup without a problem, it is very unlikely that you will experience a reaction. Try even smaller amounts of stronger drinks: a small swallow of wine or a mere sip of liquor. Many patients prefer simply to avoid alcohol rather than risk being very ill from a reaction; however, people on long-term metronidazole who hope to resume responsible drinking can minimize the risk by this gradual approach.

to sulfasalazine. Metronidazole is sometimes used to treat small-bowel Crohn's disease, although the benefit has not been proven. It does not prevent acute attacks; however, a study has shown that it can delay, and possibly decrease, recurrence of the disease after surgery.

There has been considerable enthusiasm for metronidazole, but no one has ever published a study comparing it with other antibiotics in the treatment of Crohn's disease. In the 1950s and 1960s tetracycline was used. The next drug to be popular was ampicillin. In the 1970s there was some enthusiasm for using erythromycin and cephalexin. Metronidazole was the drug of the 1980s. While it has continued to be popular, ciprofloxacin, the "new kid on the block," has also become widely used.

Side Effects of Metronidazole

By far the most common side effects of metronidazole are gastrointestinal. Nausea, decreased appetite, vomiting, constipation, diarrhea, and indigestion have all been reported, though only the first two are relatively common. Some patients complain of a constant metallic taste in the mouth. Others find that everything they eat tastes bad. The tongue may feel or even appear "furry." Continuous therapy for weeks to months can damage the nerves in the feet and legs. This shows up as persistent numbness or tingling in the feet, or difficulty with balance (clumsiness or unsteadiness), especially when walking. These effects are generally reversible, though the return to normal may take several months after the drug has been stopped.

Headaches can occur but are more likely in association with alcohol. Although most interactions with alcohol are related to drinking alcoholic beverages, sometimes someone gets headaches simply by absorbing alcohol through the skin from perfumes or colognes.

Some people who drink alcohol while on metronidazole become quite ill. Symptoms include extreme flushing of the face, shortness of breath, severe headache, rapid and pounding heartbeat, nausea and vomiting, and, occasionally, collapse. Recovery is complete following a period of drowsiness or sleep.

Ciprofloxacin in Crohn's Disease

Although few controlled studies have been done, there have been several enthusiastic reports about this antibiotic, alone or in combination with metronidazole, in people with peri-anal Crohn's disease. It is also used to treat Crohn's ileitis and/or colitis. One of the main drawbacks at the moment is its cost.

Side Effects of Ciprofloxacin

This drug is very well tolerated. The most common side effects are nausea and diarrhea, which occur in only about 1 in 100 patients. Ciprofloxacin slows down the inactivation of caffeine, prolonging and possibly increasing its stimulant effect. This does not mean that caffeine should be avoided, just that people who are sensitive to its stimulating effects should be aware of this possible increase. Some individuals have reported difficulty sleeping and vivid dreams. Drugs in this class can also cause inflammation of tendons (tendinitis) and there are rare reports of ruptured (torn) tendons, particularly the Achilles tendon.

Ciprofloxacin comes in tablets and there is an intravenous form, but the latter is usually unnecessary.

Clarithromycin

This is a member of the erythromycin family of drugs. It has been used in Crohn's disease with some success. This drug is quite well tolerated. Relatively common side effects include a bad taste and nausea. Vomiting and diarrhea are uncommon.

Other Therapies

Probiotics and Prebiotics

We are born germ-free, but our gastrointestinal system rapidly becomes colonized by bacteria and other germs from our food and environment. Some of these, known as probiotic or "friendly" bacteria, appear to play a role in keeping us healthy. When we eat foods with friendly bacteria (such as yogurt containing active culture), they can help replace "unfriendly" bacteria that may be making us ill.

Antibiotics can upset the normal bacterial population of our gastrointestinal system. Once these drugs are stopped, our bodies may not be able to restore the normal bacteria, especially if we are malnourished. Probiotics seem to help.

Many non-food probiotic products are on the market; unfortunately, their quality control tends to be poor and their safety cannot be guaranteed. One fairly new product, known as VSL-3, is believed to be reliable, but at present it is fairly expensive.

There are also foods and nutrients known as *pre*biotics, which the friendly bacteria need to maintain themselves. Honey, onions, and some grains are examples of foods containing prebiotics.

Although there have been several studies using probiotics for IBD, and many claims of benefit, so far the only really convincing study is one that showed VSL-3 to be effective in controlling pouchitis (see Chapter 7). More studies are underway.

Fish Oil

Naturally occurring chemicals known as omega-3 fatty acids have been shown to have anti-inflammatory properties. One source of these chemicals is fish oil.

One controlled study has been done in people with Crohn's disease, and it showed that more people on the fish oil stayed in remission compared to those on a placebo. A few studies have been done in ulcerative colitis, showing a modest short-term benefit. Fish oil may also help some people with arthritis, so if you have both IBD and arthritis you may receive a double benefit. Note that if you take what is considered a therapeutic amount of fish oil, you may end up smelling like fish! While this side effect is clearly not serious, it is certainly undesirable. Other side effects, which are uncommon, include nausea and diarrhea. Further studies are planned.

Lidocaine Enemas

We've known for many years that chronic bowel inflammation causes enlargement of nerve cells within the bowel wall. Researchers discovered that these nerve cells release chemicals that promote inflammation by attracting white blood cells. A Scandinavian doctor came up with the idea of putting local anesthetic into the rectums of people with ulcerative colitis. In theory, "freezing" the nerves would prevent these chemicals from being released and would stop the inflammation. No one has had the success rates this doctor claimed, but some people do respond to lidocaine enemas.

There is no lidocaine enema on the market, so you have to

get your own enema syringe and tubes of the medication, but don't do so unless it's prescribed by your doctor. This is expensive and most drug plans don't pay for it.

When used in other ways, lidocaine can cause epileptic seizures if absorbed into the bloodstream in large quantities. However, this side effect has not been reported with enema therapy. Other than that, there do not seem to be any side effects of using lidocaine in this way.

Heparin

In 1991, Dr. P. Gaffney, an Irish physician, reported on an ulcerative colitis patient who needed the anticoagulant (blood thinner) heparin for a blood clot in his leg. His colitis improved dramatically when the heparin was started. Several studies have verified that this treatment works for attacks of ulcerative colitis in some people. However, it needs to be given by injection, which is inconvenient. Side effects are uncommon; surprisingly, increased bleeding is *not* one of them. No studies on heparin as a maintenance treatment have been reported.

Short-Chain Fatty Acid Enemas

Some people with colitis limited to the left side of the colon may respond to enemas containing these naturally occurring chemicals (see Chapter 2). Other than the usual mechanical risk of having an enema, there are no side effects.

No commercial short-chain fatty-acid product exists. It is usually manufactured by hospital pharmacies at the request of a gastroenterologist. Because this is not a marketed product, drug plans do not pay for it. There is no oral form.

Cromolyn Enemas

In the mid-1970s a doctor in England reported on a group

of patients with resistant ulcerative proctitis who responded to this asthma medication when it was given directly into the rectum. There was some enthusiasm for this in selected cases of proctitis, but it is rarely used at present.

There is no enema form. You have to purchase oral capsules, dissolve the powder in the capsules in warm water, and supply your own enema syringe.

Nicotine

Nicotine protects some people against ulcerative colitis! In the mid-1980s, the following case was reported in the medical literature.

A young woman in Boston decided to quit smoking. Shortly thereafter she developed ulcerative colitis. She was referred to a gastroenterologist but proved to have a stubborn case that did not respond well to treatment. She became frustrated and started smoking again. Her colitis got better. Once she was back to normal, she quit smoking a second time. The colitis returned and was again resistant to therapy. Once again she started smoking, and the colitis settled down. She quit smoking yet another time and the colitis returned. At this point she went to her doctor and told him that every time she stopped smoking she developed colitis, and every time she started again the colitis was controlled. Her doctor wondered if it could be the nicotine, and treated her with nicotine gum, which was the only medicinal form of nicotine available at that time. She and her doctor then determined that 12 milligrams of nicotine daily controlled her colitis, but 6 milligrams daily did not.

Statistics from the Boston University hospital system and many other centers have shown that there are three times as many non-smokers as smokers with ulcerative colitis. Studies have also shown that it is not the act of stopping smoking that increases the risk; rather, it is simply the fact of becoming a nonsmoker. This means that a person who quits smoking has the same risk of developing colitis as a person who has never smoked.

How nicotine protects against ulcerative colitis is unknown. The therapeutic effect can be achieved by smoking but, considering the health hazards of smoking, this is obviously not a reasonable strategy. Nicotine-containing gum has been used, but is not popular because it is very sticky and hard to chew. It is better tolerated if it is sucked, but this is difficult to do for prolonged periods. The introduction of the nicotine patch has made this therapy more practical.

Nicotine patches are expensive and many drug plans will not pay for this form of treatment. People who have never smoked may be less likely to tolerate nicotine than those who have. Only brief (six-week) studies have been done. We don't know if long-term use of nicotine in this way is safe or effective. The most common side effects include nausea, light-headedness, headache, sleep disturbance or vivid dreams, dizziness, skin irritation due to the patch, sweating, and shaking of the hands.

If you have Crohn's disease, take note! Smoking may be protective for some people with ulcerative colitis, but it is bad for some people with Crohn's. *Stopping* smoking is beneficial to some people with Crohn's.

Further Drugs for IBD

It is beyond the scope of this book to cover *all* the treatments for IBD described in the world literature. Some of the ones still under study are: anti-TB drug combinations, MAP kinase inhibition, ISS-ODNs, extracorporeal photochemotherapy, immunoglobulin infusions, T-lymphocyte apheresis (TLA), hyperbaric oxygen, and even some herbal products.

Drugs That Reduce Symptoms without Affecting Inflammation

Certain drugs do not reduce inflammation but are used to reduce or eliminate symptoms.

Antidiarrheals

During flare-ups of IBD, most gastroenterologists prefer to avoid these drugs because complications may be more likely to occur.

But between flare-ups, many patients, especially those with Crohn's disease, are troubled by urgency, cramps, and diarrhea. The symptoms may be controlled with antidiarrheal drugs, which are generally safer than drugs that reduce symptoms by reducing inflammation.

How Do Antidiarrheal Drugs Work?

Antidiarrheal drugs work by altering the muscle activity of the small and large intestines, causing waste material to pass through more slowly.

What Are the Side Effects?

When taken between flare-ups of IBD, their main side effect is constipation, which may in turn increase abdominal pain and cause a sensation of bloating. *Do not take these drugs if you think you are having a flare-up or an obstruction, unless advised to do so by your doctor.*

The narcotic antidiarrheal medications (codeine, diphenoxylate, tincture of opium, paregoric) may also cause nausea, vomiting, drowsiness, dizziness, and itchy rashes. However, these are all very uncommon. All narcotics carry the risk of addiction, but the risk is extremely low when these drugs are used in the treatment of bowel disorders.

Loperamide is the safest of all the antidiarrheal drugs. It is chemically similar to the narcotics, but is not classified as one and is therefore available over the counter, without prescription, but it is expensive. Most drug plans will not pay for it. It is often a first choice when an antidiarrheal drug is needed. However, if cost is an issue, something that is covered by drug plans may be prescribed instead.

Not only is loperamide the safest antidiarrheal drug, but it is also long-acting, so that it usually needs to be taken only once or twice a day. In comparison, diphenoxylate, codeine, and the other narcotics usually need to be taken three or four times a day. The fewer times a medication has to be taken, the more likely it is to be taken at the right times.

Loperamide, diphenoxylate, and codeine are all available as tablets, and loperamide and codeine are also available as syrups. Tincture of opium is a liquid dosed in drops, while paregoric is a dilute solution of opium taken by the teaspoonful.

Bulk Formers
Bulk formers are drugs that bind (soak up) water in the stool, reducing looseness and sometimes frequency of stools as well. They may be thought of as commercial forms of fiber.

When are Bulk Formers Used?
Relatively mild diarrhea in both ulcerative colitis and Crohn's disease can be controlled with these products. However, bear in mind that while the stool may be more solid, it may also be more frequent, rather than less frequent.

What Are the Side Effects?
Side effects with bulk formers are very uncommon. Some individuals feel bloated and gassy. Many products give off a fine

dust when they are handled; inhaling this dust repeatedly can cause you to become allergic, and serious reactions may result. But this is extremely rare. You can avoid this by handling the products at arm's length.

Bulk formers are sold in many different flavors, as powders or granules. Most are some form of psyllium, a natural fiber source. Wheat bran can be equally effective.

Bile-Salt Binders

These drugs bind (form a chemical complex) with bile salts, a normal product of the liver. Bile salts flow, dissolved in the bile, from the liver via the bile duct to the intestine, where they aid in digesting fat. Normally, 90 to 99 percent of the bile salts are reabsorbed by the ileum and recycled. The 1 to 10 percent that reaches the colon is lost in the stool without causing any problems. However, if some of the ileum is diseased or has been removed, more of the bile salts reach the colon. The excess irritates the lining of the colon. This causes an outpouring of water into the colon, which is the opposite of what is supposed to happen (normally water is absorbed). The result is diarrhea. By forming a chemical complex with the bile salts, bile-salt binders can prevent this irritation.

When Are They Used?

Diarrhea in someone with ileal disease or previous ileal resection can be treated with these drugs. However, if the diarrhea is equally well controlled by one of the other antidiarrheals, that is perfectly acceptable medically, and may well be more acceptable to the person. These drugs are generally not used in ulcerative colitis.

What Are the Side Effects?

People on bile-salt binders may have difficulty digesting and absorbing fat. This occurs mainly in those who have extensive ileal disease, or who have had a surgical resection of more than three feet (a meter) of ileum. The vitamins A, D, E, and K are all fats, and therefore may not be absorbed normally. This can generally be treated with vitamin supplements. These vitamins can be toxic; do not take them in large amounts without consulting your doctor.

Other side effects of bile-salt binders include nausea, vomiting, constipation, abdominal pain, and bloating. Occasionally folate (a B vitamin) deficiency develops due to decreased absorption. Absorption of other medications taken at the same time may be reduced or delayed.

Cholestyramine is the only antidiarrheal bile-salt binder currently available. It comes as a powder that doesn't really dissolve in anything, and it has a metallic taste. Because cholestyramine powder is inconvenient and unpalatable, many physicians (and patients) prefer to use loperamide, diphenoxylate, or codeine for diarrhea.

Drugs for Other Problems

Hemorrhoids and Anal Fissures
Hemorrhoids that are not bleeding and not causing any other problems don't require any treatment. When hemorrhoids do need to be treated, the treatment is much the same as it is for anal fissures (see Chapter 9). If bowel movements are hard, something needs to be done to make them softer. As you can imagine, the words "hard" and "soft" mean different things to different people. A misunderstanding between a doctor and a patient can lead to making the stools excessively soft. This can be a problem because excessive softening is usually associated with increased frequency, and that is often not desirable. As a target, you should aim for one or two large, formed, easy-to-pass bowel movements

hat Can I Take If I Get Constipated uring a Colitis Flare-up?

(or people with mild colitis involving the last two feet—about half a meter— or less of the colon. It is essential that you check with your doctor before following any of these suggestions.)

If you have been constipated for four days or less, giving yourself a small enema of plain tapwater may be all that is necessary. An alternative is to use a suppository such as a glycerine suppository or, for something with a little more punch, a bisacodyl suppository.

If a suppository or enema does not "uncork" the system, you must generally take something by mouth to thoroughly soften and/or flush out the accumulated stool. The first and safest choice is to drink one or two quarts (liters) of a colonic lavage solution. These solutions are mildly salty and contain polyethylene glycol, or PEG for short. The PEG prevents the salt and water from being absorbed into the blood and the result is that the colon is flushed out. Some colonic lavage solutions are flavored. I advise my patients to drink about two cups (half a liter) an hour, or to take it even more slowly if nausea is a problem. (These directions are different from those on the container.)

The second choice (which has risks for some people) is to drink a bottle of a sodium phosphate solution. Although this solution is extremely salty, the volume is so small that most people can put up with the taste for the brief time it takes to drink it. I advise my patients to mix the phosphate solution with an equal amount of sweet juice, making a total volume of about three ounces (100 milliliters). It is a good idea to have a glass of a sweet beverage to drink right after the phosphate solution. You must drink as much clear fluid as possible – juices, broths – for the next five hours; then you can resume eating. Bowel movements will usually begin in about two hours and most people will be cleaned out within about five hours. Note that some people cannot tolerate the extremely salty phosphate solution, while others must avoid it because of its high salt content.

Roughly speaking, a bottle of phosphate solution is equivalent to two quarts (liters) of PEG–salt water solution. Whichever method you use, it is not necessary to achieve the total cleanout needed before a colonoscopy or barium enema. If the attack of colitis has been controlled, the constipation will probably not come back.

Some people should not or cannot drink either of these but do need something for the constipation that can occur during an attack of colitis. You should avoid harsh laxatives. This includes most over-the-counter brand-name laxatives. My suggestion (the third choice) in this situation is mineral oil. (A raspberry-flavored brand is available in some countries.) Take two tablespoons (30 milliliters) every two to four hours while you are awake. Eat normally. After about two days, you will usually start to pass some oil from the rectum. (You may want to put a pad or some tissue in your underwear to soak up the oil.) Continue the same dose of oil until you have had two or three large, greasy bowel movements, or ten or more smaller ones. Then reduce the oil to one tablespoon (15 milliliters) a day, in the evening, until it is clear that the attack of colitis is coming under control. At this point, you can stop the oil. The constipation should not come back.

Mineral oil is undesirable as a laxative on a regular basis. It is messy and inconvenient. Some physicians believe it can interfere with absorption of the fat-soluble vitamins (A, D, E, and K), but this is unproven.

every day, without forcing or straining. Many people can achieve this simply by increasing the amount of fiber in their diet.

In addition to regular bowel movements, it is useful to apply local medication to reduce inflammation in the area of the hemorrhoids and/or fissure. The things that work best are ointments and suppositories that contain a very small amount of a steroid, usually hydrocortisone. Both bowel regularity and local steroid medication shrink the tissues around hemorrhoids and reduce the overall swelling.

Reducing inflammation is a particularly important part of treating fissures. Inflammation in the region of the anus usually causes some spasm (excessive and persistent muscular activity) of the anal sphincter. This promotes constipation because passing stool is resisted. Constipation temporarily makes things better because the fissure can start to heal or hemorrhoids can start to shrink when nothing is passing through the anal canal and no attempt is being made to pass anything. However, whenever the sufferer decides to have a bowel movement the whole problem is aggravated, because forcing and straining will be necessary and the stool that comes out will be excessively hard.

Applying a steroid-containing ointment locally and regulating the stool are frequently adequate to treat hemorrhoids, but sometimes not enough to treat fissures. One of the simplest things you can do, and something that is very effective in relaxing the anal sphincter, is to use a sitz bath at least once a day. A sitz bath is a plastic bowl that looks much like a bedpan. It fits into your toilet and has a flange around it that rests on the edge of the bowl. The sitz bath has little overflow holes so that water in the pan does not spill onto the floor when you sit in it. All you need to do is fill it with plain warm water; you don't have to add salt or baking soda. Be careful to avoid using water that is too hot, as burning the skin will simply injure and inflame it further. Five to ten minutes per sitz bath is enough. Sitz baths are best right after a bowel movement, but many people find that the most convenient time is at bedtime. If you happen to have a bidet in your bathroom, you can use it instead.

Fissures resistant to the above treatments are now sometimes treated with nitroglycerine ointment (there is no commercial product; it is usually manufactured in hospital pharmacies) or botulinum toxin injection. Space does not permit detailed discussion of these therapies; check with your physician.

You should not use steroid-containing ointments or suppositories indefinitely, because one of the long-term side effects is a thinning of the skin, so it will actually become less resistant to irritation. Once the acute problem has subsided, continue with bowel regulation and sitz baths, as needed.

Many people are troubled by hemorrhoids or fissures as a result of chronic diarrhea rather than constipation. High-fiber diets are not usually helpful in reducing diarrhea. Your doctor is the person to consult for the best treatment of diarrhea, be it through some change in your diet or through medication.

Itching In or Around the Anus

Another complaint frequently associated with hemorrhoids is an itch in the region of the anus. This usually occurs for one or two reasons. The skin of the anal canal first becomes irritated because of frequent wiping. Once the skin is irritated, it becomes even more sensitive than usual. Stool is irritating to skin. Even when people are quite careful about wiping themselves, bits of stool are frequently left between the multiple folds of skin present in the anal canal. If you have hemorrhoids, there are even more folds where bits of stool can get trapped. The stool further inflames the already irritated skin. This results in an itch.

The treatment for an anal itch is much the same as the treatment for hemorrhoids and fissures. Controlling diarrhea is important so you won't have to wipe frequently. Cleaning the skin through the use of sitz baths is helpful because no rubbing is necessary. When you sit in the sitz bath, the anal sphincter relaxes, releasing bits of stool trapped between the folds of the anal lining. It is often helpful to apply some kind of ointment to the irritated area after the sitz bath. Initially this can be a steroid-containing ointment. Eventually what will be needed is simply something to act as a barrier to protect the skin against further irritation by stool. Zinc oxide, various baby ointments, and even petroleum jelly are all acceptable. If itching is an ongoing or frequently recurring problem, changing your toilet habits may help. After wiping off most of the residual stool following a bowel movement, fold some toilet paper, wet it, then press it onto the area around the anus. Doing this two or three times will enable you to complete cleaning the area without any rubbing. If you have diarrhea and must do this frequently, the skin will get quite dry. In this situation, apply a barrier ointment of some kind every night. If an anal itch is intense or resistant to treatment, there may be another cause. Consult your doctor!

Analgesics (Painkillers)

Occasionally you may feel you need a painkiller for symptoms not controlled by your regular medications, or for some unrelated problem – a headache, for example.

ASA, the most widely available nonprescription painkiller, is somewhat undesirable in IBD. Its chemical properties make ulcerative colitis patients bleed more when the colon is inflamed. Stomach and duodenal ulcers are more common in Crohn's disease patients than in the general population, and ASA increases the risk of getting an ulcer.

The preferred nonprescription analgesic is acetaminophen; it is available under many different names, but generic or "no-name" forms are just as good. Acetaminophen also has risks, but for the IBD patient it does not have as many as ASA. An overdose of acetaminophen can fatally injure the liver. Large doses taken for many years may cause kidney damage.

Nonsteroidal Anti-inflammatory Drugs (NSAIDs)

Some 10 to 20 percent of people with IBD experience pain in one or more joints. In some cases, simple acetaminophen is enough to relieve the pain. However, many people require drugs specifically for arthritis. These all fall into a family known as "nonsteroidal anti-inflammatory drugs" (NSAIDs), commonly referred to as "anti-inflammatories." These are currently divided into two groups: nonselective and selective.

Drugs in the first group include ibuprofen, indomethacin, naproxen, sulindac, piroxicam, ketoprofen, and diclofenac, among others. Drugs in the selective group include celecoxib, rofecoxib, valdecoxib, etoricoxib, and others.

Any of these drugs can cause inflammation of the colon (so-called NSAID colitis). This reaction is no more likely to occur in people with IBD than in those without it. It usually gets better quickly when the drug is stopped. However, there is a chance that a reaction to the drug will trigger a flare-up of the IBD. This is not an allergic reaction and it does not mean that NSAIDs must be avoided. In fact, it is not even clearly established that the same drug will cause the same reaction if it is taken again on another occasion. Early data suggest that this reaction is less likely with the selective NSAIDs.

Other Side Effects of NSAIDs

Up to 25 percent of people taking NSAIDs experience burning discomfort in the upper abdomen or behind the breastbone (heartburn), or some other form of indigestion. People with a history of acid-related problems and people over 60 are much more prone to this. Other relatively common side effects are nausea and allergic reactions. The risk of ulcers in the stomach or duodenum from taking these medications can be reduced by using misoprostol at the same time, but a common side effect of that drug is diarrhea. Better protection with fewer side effects is achieved with proton pump inhibitors such as omeprazole, pantoprazole, lansoprazole, or rabeprazole, but these drugs are expensive. The risk of ulcers is much less when the selective NSAIDs are used, and protection may not be needed.

Some NSAIDs come in slow-release forms or are long-acting and can be taken once or twice a day. Others need to be taken three or four times a day. The slow-release forms can cause ulceration and even perforation of the small intestine and colon. Because at least one of those areas is already abnormal in someone with IBD, there may be a greater risk of this happening.

Although some people must take these drugs continuously for months or even years, using them intermittently is preferable, if possible. Most arthritis associated with IBD does not damage or destroy joints, so getting rid of the inflammation is not essential. See if you can control minor aches and pains with acetaminophen, which is considerably safer.

Antibiotics

As discussed earlier, some antibiotics are used to treat some people for Crohn's disease. But you may need antibiotics for other conditions. It is comforting to know that such antibiotics are no more likely to cause adverse effects in people with IBD than in other individuals. They should be prescribed and taken when needed. But remember that antibiotics occasionally cause a form of colitis due to an overgrowth of a bacterium named *Clostridium difficile* (*C. diff* for short). It's usually fairly easy to distinguish between colitis due to IBD and antibiotic-associated colitis, though. If you are having an attack of colitis, always tell your gastroenterologist if you are on antibiotics, or have been within the past few months.

Acid-Reducing Drugs

"Heartburn," a burning sensation felt behind the breastbone or in the upper abdomen just below the breastbone, is usually due to a condition called reflux esophagitis, in which stomach acid backs up into the esophagus. Millions of people in the world have it, including many people with IBD. The most effective therapy is to reduce the amount of acid produced by the stomach. All the drugs in this category have few side effects and can be taken with any of the standard therapies for IBD.

The best-known acid-reducing drugs are in a family known as histamine-2-receptor antagonists (also known as H-2 blockers). They include cimetidine, ranitidine, famotidine, and nizatidine.

Proton pump inhibitors (such as omeprazole, pantoprazole, lansoprazole, and rabeprazole) are the most potent acid-suppressing medications. However, they are also the most expensive, and are not always necessary. Stomach acid has the important protective function of killing the germs we take in with food. Therefore suppressing the production of acid just enough to relieve your symptoms is preferable.

Iron
Iron-deficiency anemia is a common problem in IBD (see Chapter 9). If it develops, most patients will require supplemental iron.

Iron tablets come in many forms. Commonly used products include ferrous sulfate and ferrous gluconate. Common side effects of taking iron supplements are nausea and a change in bowel habit. Some people get diarrhea; others get constipated. Sometimes these side effects cause enough trouble that the dose has to be reduced or the medication even stopped. All patients on supplemental iron notice that their stools are darker, since much of the iron in each pill is not absorbed. Stools may even appear black.

If you have unacceptable side effects with even one iron tablet a day, try a combination of a small amount of an iron-containing syrup and a high-iron diet (see below).

If you cannot get enough iron by mouth, you'll have to get it by injection, either intramuscularly (into muscle) or intravenously (into a vein). Absorption of iron from medication or food is very limited. Your doctor can monitor the need with blood tests. Do not take iron pills or high-iron foods indefinitely without your doctor's agreement.

High-Iron Foods

	Serving size	Iron (mg)
Meat and alternates		
Pork liver, cooked	3 oz (90 gm)	26.1
Beef kidney, cooked	3 oz (90 gm)	11.8
Beef, chicken liver, cooked	3 oz (90 gm)	8.0
Baked beans with pork and tomato sauce	1 cup (250 mL)	4.9
Chili with beans	1 cup (250 mL)	4.5
Corned beef	3 oz (90 gm)	3.9
Liverwurst	2 oz (60 gm)	3.2
Seeds: pumpkin, sesame	1/4 cup (50 mL)	3.2
Beef, pork, veal, ham – roasted	3 oz (90 gm)	3.0
Fruits and vegetables		
Prune juice	1/2 cup (125 mL)	5.5
Spinach (cooked)	1/2 cup (125 mL)	3.4
Cereals		
Whole-grain and dry enriched	3/4 cup (200 mL)	4.5

Advantages and Disadvantages of Intramuscular Iron Injections:
- given at the doctor's office;
- should be given into large muscle mass;
- multiple injections are necessary;
- immediate side effects include pain at the injection site and allergic reactions, occasionally severe;
- risk of side effects increased if iron pills are also being taken.

Advantages and Disadvantages of Intravenous Iron Injections:
- a large muscle mass is not necessary (many IBD patients are underweight);
- not painful;
- usually given in hospital setting;
- unfamiliar to many doctors.

The most important thing about receiving iron injections, either intramuscularly or intravenously, is to be sure that this form of supplementation is truly necessary.

Recombinant Erythropoietin
Chronic diseases can suppress bone marrow function so that even if all the building blocks (one of them being iron) are available, red blood cell production may be reduced. (This condition is called anemia.) Erythropoietin is a natural substance that stimulates red blood cell production. You may feel more energetic, but there is no effect on the disease itself.

Calcium
People on low-lactose diets may need a calcium supplement. For more information, see Chapter 5.

Other Minerals
Chronic diarrhea results in deficiencies of elements needed in trace amounts by the body. People who require total parenteral nutrition (see Chapter 5) are often given supplemental zinc. Occasionally, someone will require extra chromium.

Vitamins
Many patients ask, "Do I need vitamin pills?" When the diet is restricted in some way for prolonged periods, some vitamin supplementation may be advisable. People on an enteral diet and those on total parenteral nutrition usually receive adequate amounts of both vitamins and minerals (see Chapter 5).

"Miracles" and Myths – The Placebo Effect
Characteristically, most chronic inflammatory diseases may get better or worse on their own. This can make any treatment

Complementary and Alternative Therapies

The term "complementary" is usually used for treatments such as massage, tai chi, relaxation techniques, and the like. Complementary therapies that help you feel more relaxed, stronger, and more in control of your life are helpful and safe.

The name "alternative" is generally used to describe treatments based on naturopathy, homeopathy, and related fields. While alternative medicine clearly helps some people feel better, be careful when such treatments involve prescription of herbs or other "natural" products.

It is important to realize that herbal drugs are simply drugs that come from plants. Digoxin, the heart medication, comes from the fox-glove plant; taxol, a very valuable drug for ovarian cancer, comes from the Pacific yew tree; vincristine, a drug for leukemia, comes from the vinca plant; and ASA was originally an extract of willow bark. In other words, there is nothing exclusive about the use of medicines derived from plants.

But there are important differences between most herbal products and conventional drugs derived from plants. Conventional drugs are puri-fied and studied carefully before being approved by regulatory agencies. Side-effect profiles are established. Because we know that new side effects, undetected during pre-market testing, can still arise, there are ongoing surveillance and reporting mechanisms to protect the public as much as possible. This arrangement is not perfect, but our desire for absolute safety must be balanced by our need for better treatments for many diseases.

With most herbal products, you don't know if what's on the label is what's in the bottle, and you don't know if what's in the bottle is pure. For example, a few years ago kelp products were popular. Some of them turned out to contain significant amounts of arsenic, and there were several cases of arsenic poisoning. Among other risks, liver cancer can result from excessive intake of arsenic.

But the most important issue is that of safety. You should assume that anything that can benefit you may also have risks (side effects). Because (at the time of writing) there is no government regulation requiring makers of herbal products to test their products scientifically, we simply don't know the risks of taking most herbal products.

This does not mean that such products can't help some people; it's just that you can't assume they are safe because someone tells you they are. Over the years, many herbal products have been taken off the market after serious, sometimes fatal side effects were discovered.

look effective or ineffective. For this reason, carefully controlled studies are desirable. When patients are seriously ill, we cannot ethically give some of them a placebo (a substance known to have no therapeutic effect) if proven therapies are available. However, there are many situations in which temporarily withholding active treatment is acceptable, especially in the context of controlled clinical trials.

Such studies have taught us that over a four-month period 25 to 40 percent of Crohn's patients with symptoms worthy of treatment gradually get better *without* specific "active" therapy. About 20 percent of these patients remain well for one year, and 10 percent stay well for two years. In addition, many patients whose disease is brought under control *with* active therapy remain well off treatment for one or two years or more. Findings are similar for people with ulcerative colitis. People receiving placebos may feel better for psychological reasons; if they think they are receiving a real treatment, they want it to work, and this positive attitude may be beneficial.

Whenever the cause of a chronic, incurable disease is unknown, you can expect all sorts of treatments and "cures" to be promoted. Some will be touted by people who really believe in whatever they are promoting, even if they have nothing to gain. Other treatments are put forward by individuals or groups trying to "make a buck." When people are both ill and poorly informed, they may become desperate, and this makes them susceptible to being taken in.

It is important to keep the placebo effect in mind as you read the next section.

Unorthodox Therapies
Over the years, claims of dramatic success have been made for a wide variety of unorthodox therapies, sometimes on the basis of scanty reliable information.

In the 1970s, two researchers in New York maintained that a protein isolated from the pituitary gland of cows could control diarrhea in patients with Crohn's disease. In the 1980s, a company in the U.S.A. promoted a product made from the ground-up tracheas (windpipes) of cows. In the late 1980s, two researchers in Canada claimed that a naturally occurring compound known as N-acetyl glucosamine was beneficial to patients with inflammatory bowel disease. Some people have asserted that patients with IBD can be greatly helped by "orthomolecular" medicine, meaning treatment with multiple vitamins and minerals.

These are just a few examples. Until the true causes of IBD are known, unorthodox treatments will continue to be promoted. We should keep an open mind about such ideas. Some may turn out to be valuable. However, because of the placebo effect, we should insist on carefully controlled, scientifically sound studies to evaluate any new proposed treatments, and view unsubstantiated claims with great suspicion. You might say, "If this has no risk, why shouldn't I try it?" Anything that has biological activity is likely also to have biological risk. The idea that avoiding standard therapies means avoiding risk is faulty. When you need treatment and you avoid it, there is a significant risk that the disease or complication will get worse, and may even endanger your life.

As I have said elsewhere in this book, by all means participate in your care. But do it in conjunction with your doctor.

SEVEN

Surgery for IBD

Many people think of surgery for inflammatory bowel disease as a last resort. Except for a few cases, it is not. Surgery is one of the important forms of treatment for IBD. Sometimes it's the best choice. Sometimes it's the only choice.

Using technical terms is unavoidable when discussing the various operations. Let's define some of the most common ones. You can also refer to the glossary at the back of the book.

In medical terminology, the suffix -*ectomy* means removal. A *colectomy* is removal of the colon. *Total colectomy* (also known as *proctocolectomy*; *procto-* from the Latin word *proctum*, which means "rectum") is removal of the colon, including the rectum. To do this, the anus must also be removed. *Proctectomy* means removal of the rectum.

Another technical term for this is *abdominoperineal resection*, indicating that it is really two operations combined into one. Incisions must be made in both the abdomen and the perineum. The term *perineum* refers to the area between the anus and genitals.

Subtotal colectomy means removing all of the colon except the rectum. In the following pages, I use the term *near-total colectomy*, which means removing all of the colon and most of the rectum. It is not a standard term but is useful in explaining and understanding some of the operations.

The suffix *-ostomy* refers to a surgically created connection between a hollow organ and the skin, or between two hollow organs. *Resect* means cut out. *Anastomosis* refers to a surgically created connection. An *ileostomy* is an opening of the ileum out to the skin; a *colostomy* is the same thing using the colon. The plastic bag that fits over the opening at the skin, or *stoma* (meaning "mouth"), is called an appliance. The appliance is attached to a plastic ring that is kept in position on the abdominal wall by an adhesive paste. All ostomies, with one exception (see Kock ileostomy, below), require the wearing of an appliance.

Surgery for Ulcerative Colitis
About a third of all people with ulcerative colitis will undergo removal of the colon during their lifetime. This is for two main reasons: because medical therapy has failed to control the disease adequately; or because precancerous changes, or actual cancer, have been found in the colon.The best way to understand the various operations for ulcerative colitis is to review the history of surgery for this disease.

The 1930s and 1940s – Subtotal Colectomy, Ileostomy, and Mucous Fistula of the Rectum
In the thirties and forties, surgical techniques and peri-operative care (peri-operative refers to the time before, during, and soon after surgery) were not nearly as good as they are now. Patients undergoing a total colectomy had many complications and a significant chance of dying as a result of this surgery. The favored operation for colitis in those days was a subtotal colectomy (removal of the colon but not the

rectum), with an ileostomy (artificial opening of the ileum out onto the abdomen) and a mucous fistula of the rectum (top of the rectum opening onto the abdomen). The rectum was not attached to the ileum, so the stool came out via the ileostomy.

The rectum was often severely inflamed in people having this surgery, and if the surgeon tried simply to sew up the top of the rectum, the stitches would often not hold and the contents of the rectum would leak into the abdomen – a dangerous complication. Surgeons figured out that if they brought the top of the rectum out to the skin, much like an ileostomy but smaller, such complications could be avoided. "Mucous fistula of the rectum" is the name for this procedure.

Making an Ileostomy

When ileostomies were first done, the *serosa* of the ileum was simply sewn to the skin. (The serosa is the outer lining of the intestine and is much like the tough casing around a hot dog or a sausage.) This was easy to do, but unfortunately it did not work very well. Because the body likes to close all unnatural openings, this type of ileostomy gradually became narrower and narrower in most cases. Scar tissue forms when healing takes place, and scar tissue shrinks with the passage of time. If the scar tissue is in the form of a ring – as it is in an ileostomy – when the ring shrinks, the outlet narrows. Patients would frequently develop an obstruction at the ileostomy and have to be operated on again, often more than once.

The 1950s – The Brooke Ileostomy

In 1952, a British surgeon named Bryan Brooke solved the above problem by devising what has become known as the Brooke ileostomy. Brooke figured that if the end of the ileum was folded over (much the way the end of a sleeve is folded

Brooke Ileostomy and Mucous Fistula of the Rectum

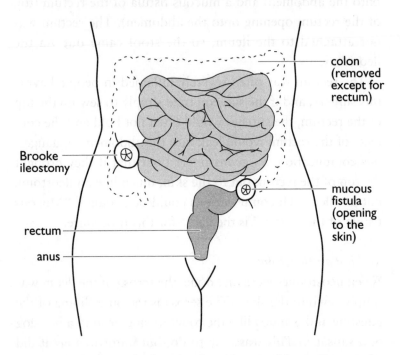

colon (removed except for rectum)

Brooke ileostomy

mucous fistula (opening to the skin)

rectum

anus

over) and *then* attached to the skin, this would usually stop the ileostomy opening from shrinking and narrowing. He was right, and the success rate for ileostomies improved dramatically. In fact, this operation has stood the test of time and is still the standard technique for creating an ileostomy.

Problems Associated with Brooke Ileostomies

Although the majority of Brooke ileostomies are trouble-free, about 25 percent of patients will have problems. There is obviously a need for a psychological adjustment; this is frequently a major social issue in school-age and unmarried people. In terms of physical activity, the only restriction relates to deep sea diving — you are not allowed to go down more than 110 feet (33 meters)! Structural abnormalities can occur in and around the ileostomy, often needing surgical repair. Some people develop skin reactions to the stool, the appliance, or the adhesives. Infection with a fungus is fairly common if the skin becomes raw, but this can be easily treated with an anti-fungal ointment. Leakage and odor are also possibilities that create concern. These problems can usually be treated by enterostomal therapists, nurses specializing in teaching patients about ostomies of various kinds. They are also specialists in solving various mechanical problems and skin irritation related to ostomies.

Many people with ileostomies must avoid high-roughage foods such as popcorn, nuts, sprouts, oranges, and grapefruit, or they may experience episodes of crampy abdominal pain.

As well, people with ileostomies need to pay attention to their fluid intake. Because output from the ileostomy contains more water than normal stool, not taking in enough fluids will result in less urine and an increased risk of kidney stones. You should always maintain a higher-than-normal fluid and salt intake, and be particularly careful to avoid becoming dehydrated if diarrhea occurs for any reason. A simple way to judge if you're dehydrated is to pay attention to urine output. If you have to urinate only once or twice a day and/or the volume of urine passed is small or the urine is unusually dark, you are likely dehydrated. If you urinate four or five times a day and/or urine volumes each time are large, and/or the urine is color-less or very pale yellow, dehydration is likely not a problem.

The 1950s – The Aylett Procedure

Another British surgeon, by the name of Aylett, devised a new operation in the 1950s. He felt that it was unnecessary to leave people with an ileostomy. He proposed a subtotal colectomy, with anastomosis (connection) of the ileum to the rectum, so that bowel movements would occur in the normal way. He performed this operation on some 300 people and reported excellent results in about 250 of them. Unfortunately, no one else could achieve results anything like Aylett's. In the hands of most surgeons, individuals who had this type of surgery continued to have very frequent bowel movements, with great urgency and incontinence (involuntary passage of stool). As a result, the operation did not achieve widespread popularity. This operation remains a potential choice if you have ulcerative colitis with minimal rectal disease and reasonably normal rectal capacity.

The 1960s – The Kock Pouch (Kock Ileostomy, Continent Ileostomy)

In the late 1960s, a Swedish surgeon named Nils Kock came up with the idea of a continent ileostomy. "Continent" means that the patient controls the emptying of the ileostomy. (We don't refer to a Brooke ileostomy as an "incontinent ileostomy" – meaning the patient has no control over the emptying – but that's really what it is.)

Kock devised the *ileal pouch* or reservoir, which he constructed by sewing together two sections of ileum, each about six inches (15 centimeters) long. He determined that such a pouch would need a capacity of about two cups (half a liter) to act like a rectum and adequately store stool.

Kock then also devised the "nipple valve." This uses the end of the ileum to create an ileostomy that acts like a one-way valve. This valve prevents stool from coming out of the ileum on its own. When you want to empty the pouch or reservoir, you insert a tube through the nipple valve into the pouch and lean forward, and the reservoir empties through the tube into the toilet. You then pull the tube out, clean it, and put it away for next time. Individuals having this surgery

A Kock Pouch and Ileostomy and Drainage of the Pouch

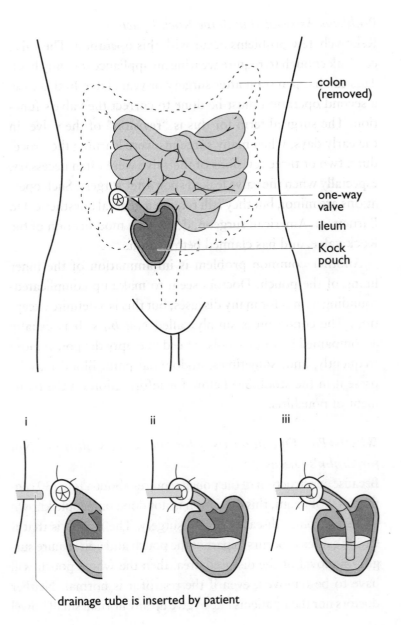

colon (removed)

one-way valve

ileum

Kock pouch

i   ii   iii

drainage tube is inserted by patient

have a total proctocolectomy at the same time, removing the colon and rectum.

Problems Associated with the Kock Pouch

Relatively few problems occur with this operation. The valve can leak enough to require wearing an appliance (ostomy bag). This can happen soon after surgery or years later. In this case, a second operation must be done to correct the valve's function. The surgical term for this is "revision" of the valve. In the early days, when many surgeons were learning the procedure, two or three revisions of the valve were often necessary, especially when the valve leaked soon after surgery. Such operations are minor, but they still require a general anesthetic. Dr. Barnett, an American surgeon, designed a modification of the Kock valve, and has claimed better results.

Another common problem is inflammation of the inner lining of the pouch. Doctors seem to make up complicated-sounding names for many diseases, but this is a definite exception. The condition is simply called *pouchitis*. It is usually accompanied by loose stools, a need to empty the pouch more frequently, and, sometimes, abdominal pain. Blood may be present in the stool. See below for information on the treatment of pouchitis.

Why Is This Operation Used for Ulcerative Colitis but Not for Crohn's Disease?

Because construction of the pouch requires about a foot (30 centimeters) of ileum, this operation is not done on people known to have Crohn's disease prior to surgery. The reason is that if Crohn's disease occurs in part of the pouch and you require surgical removal of the diseased area, then the whole pouch will have to be removed, even if the rest of it is normal. Neither doctors nor their patients like to give up any normal small bowel

in Crohn's disease. However, this operation may b(
in selected patients with Crohn's confined to the col(

Care of the Kock Ileostomy

If you have a properly functioning Kock pouch and nipple valve, you will experience little inconvenience. Many people wear a small dressing over the ileostomy to absorb the minor amount of mucus and other intestinal fluids produced locally by the mucosa (inner lining). There are no absolute dietary restrictions, but some individuals have difficulty with indigestibles such as seeds, apple skins, and celery fibers. After you have fully recovered from surgery, there are no restrictions on activity. And there are no special problems associated with pregnancy.

If you have a Kock pouch with a continent ileostomy and are troubled by frequent pouchitis or repeated difficulties with a leaky valve, then you can have surgery and change to a Brooke ileostomy. This happens to about one-third of people with a continent ileostomy.

The Present – The Pelvic Pouch with Ileo-Anal Anastomosis
It didn't take long for surgeons to realize that Kock's idea could be combined with Aylett's, to create a pouch in the pelvis with the end of the ileum attached to the anus to allow "normal" bowel movements. This "pelvic pouch with ileo-anal anastomosis" operation was introduced in the late seventies, and has become the procedure of choice for most patients undergoing surgery for ulcerative colitis.

However, the operation is generally not offered to people above the age of 65 or so. The reason is that the anal sphincter muscle in older people tends to be weaker, and these individuals are much more likely to be troubled by incontinence of stool. People who have this operation at a younger age seem able to adapt better. For older patients, the best operation for ulcerative colitis is usually a total proctocolectomy and Brooke ileostomy, which requires wearing an appliance. If such a patient is ill or malnourished, or is unwell because of other medical conditions, the best operation is a subtotal colectomy with a Brooke ileostomy and a mucous fistula of the rectum. The rectum may be removed at a later date. In some centers, age alone is not reason enough to refuse someone a pelvic-pouch operation.

How Is the Pelvic-Pouch Operation Done?
The pelvic-pouch operation can be done as a three-stage procedure, a two-stage procedure, or a one-stage procedure. When a surgeon tells you that you are going to have a three-stage operation, you should understand that this means you are going to have three operations. It's easy to understand why surgeons prefer to say a "three-stage operation" – many people would be frightened to death if they had to think about having three operations for one problem. Nevertheless, that is actually what happens.

The Three-Stage Operation
If someone with ulcerative colitis is ill and requires surgery, it will most likely be a three-stage procedure. In the first stage you will have a subtotal colectomy, construction of a Brooke ileostomy, and a mucous fistula of the rectum. Someone in this situation will almost certainly be on steroids, and likely other medications as well. Following the operation, you will be allowed to recover and your medications will be tapered off and stopped. After an interval of three to six months, the second stage will be done. Some people are anxious to get rid of the ileostomy (and the appliance) as soon as possible. But results following the second stage are better if you have

Pelvic Pouch Procedure with Ileo-Anal Anastomosis

First Stage

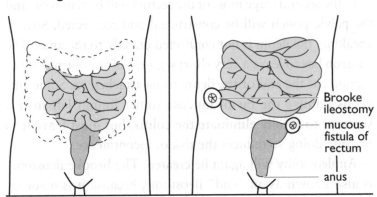

Brooke ileostomy

mucous fistula of rectum

anus

Second Stage

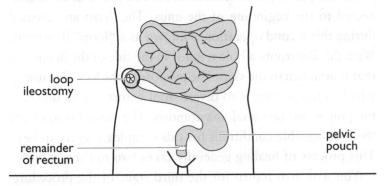

loop ileostomy

remainder of rectum

pelvic pouch

Third Stage

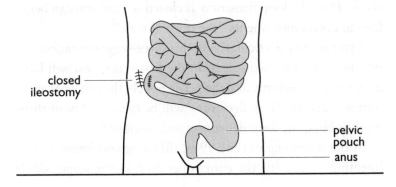

closed ileostomy

pelvic pouch

anus

regained full health and are off most or all medications, especially steroids.

In the second stage most of the rectum will be removed, and the pelvic pouch will be constructed and connected. Strictly speaking, the ileum is not connected directly to the anus. The surgeon has to leave a very short segment of the bottom of the rectum for the end of the ileum to be attached to. Some surgeons remove the bit of mucosa (inner lining) left in this segment to totally eliminate the colitis, but most leave it in because doing so reduces the risk of incontinence.

An ileostomy will again be created. The Brooke ileostomy is also known as an "end" ileostomy, because it is made by bringing the end of the ileum out through the abdominal wall. When the pelvic pouch is created, the end of the ileum is connected to the beginning of the anus. The ileostomy created during this second operation is known as a "loop" ileostomy. With this ileostomy a hole is made in the side of the ileum and that is attached to the skin. The purpose of the loop ileostomy, which is temporary, is to divert stool before it gets down to the pouch and ileo-anal anastomosis. The reason is to create the best possible conditions for this complex surgery to heal. This process of healing generally takes two to three months.

You will then return for the third stage of the procedure. This is a minor operation, but it still requires a general anesthetic. Here the loop ileostomy is closed so that you can begin having bowel movements "the normal way."

If you are not particularly ill, this three-stage operation can be combined into two stages. In the first stage, you will have a near-total colectomy and the pelvic pouch, the ileo-anal anastomosis, and the loop ileostomy will be created. About three months later, the loop ileostomy will be closed.

At the beginning of the 1990s, IBD surgeons began experimenting with doing the entire operation in one stage. While this is appealing, more patients have postsurgical complications than among those with the temporary loop ileostomy. With further experience and further improvements in technique perhaps the one-stage operation will become commonplace, but at this point it is not recommended for most people.

Side Effects and Complications of Pelvic-Pouch Surgery
This surgery involves the risk of several side effects and complications.

Frequent and/or urgent bowel movements: Pelvic-pouch surgery allows you a return to health, but many people still have an *average* of four to six semiformed bowel movements a day and one movement per night. This varies considerably – some people have ten to twelve per 24 hours, or even more. You may be much better off taking regular doses of either loperamide or diphenoxylate (see Chapter 6), with supplemental doses as necessary. Even without antidiarrheal drugs, urgency is not a problem for most patients.

Incontinence: If someone with a pelvic pouch has frequent, unpredictable bowel movements, with episodes of incontinence, little has been achieved, even though the colitis is cured. Initially many people have quite frequent stools and some degree of urgency. A small number are troubled by incontinence during the day. A somewhat larger number are troubled by incontinence that occurs only at night. The reason for this difference is that everyone passes gas from the rectum while asleep. If there is less-than-normal sensitivity in the anal canal, and particularly if loose stool is present, the gas may be accompanied by a small amount of fluid without you being aware of it. Many people wear a pad at night; only a few need to wear one during the day. Some people have more than a little incontinence of stool, and this is a major problem.

Fortunately, a significant degree of adaptation occurs during the first three to six months following the operation. The pouch gets larger and "learns" to store stool, acting like a rectum. As this happens, the daily number of trips to the bathroom usually decreases, and incontinence also decreases. Still, many people continue to wear a pad at night for psychological comfort, even after the incontinence is gone.

If incontinence remains a major problem, there is usually little choice but to give up the pelvic pouch. You can then have a Kock ileostomy; or, to have the best chance of not needing any further surgery, you can have a Brooke ileostomy. Aside from the need for psychological adjustment to the idea of a permanent stoma, the main disadvantage of the conversion to a Brooke ileostomy is that you have to lose about eighteen inches (45 cm) of healthy ileum, as the pouch cannot be taken apart.

Pouchitis: Whether you have a Kock pouch higher up in the abdomen in combination with a continent ileostomy or a pelvic pouch with an ileo-anal anastomosis, pouchitis (inflammation of the pouch) is a common problem. Most cases respond well to antibiotics; the one most commonly used is metronidazole. Budesonide enemas are also effective. Recent studies have shown that we can often prevent pouchitis from coming back by using the probiotic product VSL-3 (see Chapter 5). The cause of pouchitis is unknown. Persistent pouchitis raises the possibility of Crohn's disease.

Sexual dysfunction and fertility: Most people report that sexual function is unchanged or improved following surgery. Improvement usually reflects better general health. However, of men having this surgery, 1 to 2 percent become impotent or are unable to reach orgasm after surgery; about 4 percent experience retrograde ejaculation, which means that the semen goes into the bladder instead of coming out of the penis. In women, frequency of intercourse and ability to reach orgasm tend to increase after surgery, and painful intercourse decreases. No sex-specific problems have been reported in women after surgery.

Female fertility rates in ulcerative colitis are accepted to be normal up to the time of surgery. A Swedish group has recently reported that female fertility after the pelvic-pouch operation is reduced. Dense scar tissue formation involving the ovaries and/or fallopian tubes may be the reason. In vitro fertilization (IVF) is an option for those women who are unable to conceive within a reasonable time after full recovery from surgery.

Narrowing of the anastomosis: Some people make more scar tissue than others. Because in this case the scar tissue encircles a tube, its inevitable shrinkage during healing may produce narrowing.

In about 5 percent of patients undergoing ileo-anal anastomosis, a stricture (narrowing) develops at the site of the anastomosis. This can usually be treated by dilatation (stretching), which is a simple procedure done with a local anesthetic and/or sedative, but usually not requiring a general anesthetic.

Postoperative leak: Postoperative leak happens occasionally with any type of bowel surgery, and does not reflect badly on the surgeon. If a leak occurs, an abscess (boil) is likely to form next to the anastomosis. This will result in pain in the pelvis or around the anus, and fever. The abscess will generally require drainage, either by inserting a very fine needle into it to extract the pus, or by making a small cut into the abscess with a scalpel so the pus can drain on its own. Sometimes infection due to a leak will clear up simply with antibiotic therapy.

Inflammation at the anastomosis (recently named "cuffitis"): Because most people are left with a tiny piece (like a cuff) of rectal lining, it is possible to have persistent or recurrent colitis in this area. About 10 percent of people will have symptoms, such as urgency or bleeding. Treatment with 5-ASA or hydrocortisone suppositories is usually effective.

Who Can Have a Kock Pouch and Ileostomy?

The Kock (continent) ileostomy is an alternative to the Brooke ileostomy for certain ulcerative colitis patients in the following groups:

- those with a Brooke ileostomy who have had a total proctocolectomy and who wish to avoid wearing an appliance;
- those who need a colectomy but are not candidates for a pelvic pouch, usually because of poor anal-sphincter function;
- those who prefer a continent ileostomy to a pelvic pouch with ileo-anal anastomosis – usually people who cannot make frequent trips to the bathroom because of their jobs;
- those who have had a failed ileo-anal anastomosis but still prefer continence to wearing an external appliance.

Cancer: Cancer of the colon occurs more commonly in people with ulcerative colitis than it does in the general population. When the whole colon is removed (total proctocolectomy), the risk is removed. When a person undergoes a pouch procedure with an ileo-anal anastomosis, a tiny cuff of colon (the last bit of the rectum) is usually left in. Even if the surgeon peels off whatever can be seen of the inner lining of the colon, it is always possible that a few microscopic glands will be left behind. These glands could at some point give rise to a cancer. With the shift to leaving the mucosa (inner lining) intact, the risk is slightly greater, but overall it is still extremely low.

Indeterminate Colitis

We are unable to distinguish ulcerative colitis from Crohn's disease in about 10 percent of patients. In most centers, if surgery is needed, such patients are given the benefit of the doubt and are offered a pelvic-pouch procedure with ileo-anal anastomosis. However, they should understand that the chances that this operation will fail are higher than they are for people with clearcut ulcerative colitis. Still, the chances of success are reasonably good. If the problem is in fact ulcerative colitis, the failure rate will be no more than usual. If it is Crohn's disease, about 65 percent of people will be disease-free ten years later.

Surgery for Crohn's Disease

Surgery for ulcerative colitis involves removing most or all of the colon. Surgery for Crohn's disease depends on where in the GI tract the disease occurs.

People with Crohn's disease require surgery for three main reasons: the failure of medical therapy to control the disease adequately; chronic or frequently recurring obstructions; and abscesses with or without fistulas (abnormal channels).

The decision that medical therapy has failed to control the disease adequately, and that surgery is needed, should be made jointly by the gastroenterologist, the surgeon, and the patient (or patient's parents). The criteria may be different for different people.

Obstructions

You can think of the intestine as an elastic band. It has a thin wall; the opening is large in relation to the thickness of the wall, and it is able to stretch easily. When Crohn's disease occurs in the intestine, the wall becomes swollen. It swells outward, but it also swells inward. Now the intestine is more like a tire. It is still somewhat stretchy, but the wall is thicker and stiffer and the channel is much narrower.

During an acute obstruction, the swelling increases even more. The wall swells outward more (which is not a problem) but it also swells inward more. The intestinal channel does not have to be completely blocked to act blocked. If someone with acute small-bowel obstruction goes on a clear-fluid diet or

Thickening of Intestinal Wall

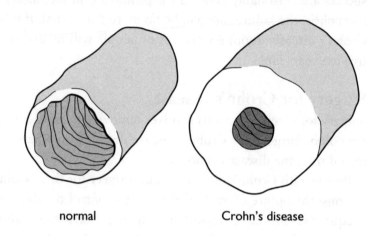

normal   Crohn's disease

takes prednisone, the swelling will almost always decrease and the obstruction will get better, usually within 48 hours.

If the person begins to have frequently recurring obstructions or has some symptoms of obstruction all the time (nausea, bloating, and crampy abdominal pain soon after every meal), the narrowing of the intestine is likely due not only to swelling, but also to scarring. Steroids or an enteral (sterilized liquid) diet should reduce the swelling. But when the narrowing is due mainly to scarring, no drug or diet treatment will relieve the problem for long, if at all.

An area of scarring may be dilated (stretched) with an inflatable balloon passed through an endoscope, if the area can be reached with a scope. Improvements in equipment have raised the success rate in experienced hands from 20 percent to as high as 75 percent, with relief of obstructive symptoms for a year or more.

There are two types of surgery for small-bowel Crohn's disease: strictureplasty and resection. *Strictureplasty* comes from *stricture*, meaning narrowing, and *-plasty*, meaning shaping something through the use of surgery. You can think of the procedure as plastic surgery on the intestine. *Resection* means removing something by cutting it out.

The idea in strictureplasty is to take a narrowed area of intestine and make it wider. People with Crohn's disease of the small bowel who should be considered for this type of surgery fall into two groups: those who have had a previous resection and need another operation, and those who need surgery and have never had it before, but have very extensive disease. Some people undergoing strictureplasty also require resection of additional segments of diseased intestine that are not suitable for strictureplasty.

Most people who undergo strictureplasty are later able to stop taking most or all medications, eat normally, and gain weight. In long-term follow-up, the majority of strictures that are opened in this way remain open. When people who have had strictureplasty require surgery for obstruction again, it is usually due to the formation of new strictures.

What is interesting about this surgery is that the Crohn's disease in the area of the operated-on stricture improves considerably after the operation. When strictureplasty patients are operated upon for some other reason, the areas of strictureplasty usually appear much less inflamed than before the strictureplasty. We can conclude that, while the disease itself causes the narrowing, the narrowing somehow makes the disease worse.

Surgery for Crohn's of the Ileum
Although Crohn's disease is often referred to as a segmental or patchy disease, in most people the disease occurs at the end of the ileum, with or without involving the beginning of the colon. When such people require surgery for the first time, they have a resection of the area of the disease with anastomosis

Strictureplasty

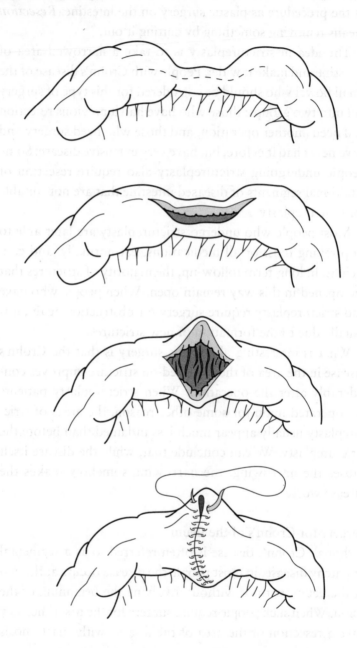

(connection) of the new end of the ileum to the ascending colon in one of two ways. This is generally a simple, straightforward operation. It's just like cutting out the middle of a shirtsleeve and sewing the lower end to the upper end.

Some people having a resection have one or more fistulas from the area of disease to another part of the intestine which is not affected by Crohn's disease. The surgeon may have to remove a little piece of intestine where the fistula runs in. If you have such a fistula and it leads to the rectum, you may need a temporary colostomy to divert the stool away from the site of the repaired fistula, allowing the rectum to rest and heal properly. In a minor operation, the colostomy will be closed two to three months later.

Common Side Effects of Resection of the End of the Ileum
Removing the end of the ileum is not without consequences. These include:

- *Diarrhea due to loss of the ileocecal valve:* The ileocecal valve allows liquid intestinal contents to be discharged into the colon in a controlled, intermittent fashion. Surgical removal can lead to diarrhea. This effect is almost always temporary.
- *Bile-salt diarrhea:* Normally, 90 to 99 percent of bile salts reaching the ileum are recycled back to the liver and reused. The remaining 1 to 10 percent are lost into the colon. When even a bit of ileum is removed, the amount lost each day into the colon is increased.

  Certain bile salts have a laxative-like effect on the colon, and the colon loses salt and water instead of absorbing them as it is supposed to. The result is diarrhea. Fortunately, bile-salt diarrhea is usually easy to control with drugs (see Chapter 6).

Surgery for the Most Common Form of Crohn's Disease

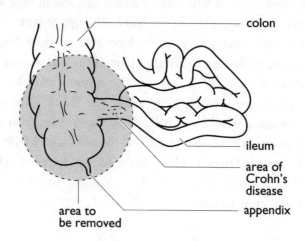

colon

ileum

area of
Crohn's
disease

appendix

area to
be removed

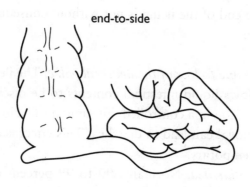

end-to-side

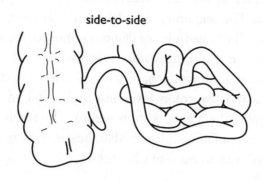

side-to-side

- *Decreased fat digestion and absorption:* When you undergo resection (removal) of more than about a yard (a meter) of the end of the ileum, two things happen. First, the liver is unable to maintain a normal level of bile salts in the intestine to digest fat. Second, large resections such as this interfere with absorption of the fat that is digested, because fat requires the greatest length of intestine for its absorption.

  If cholestyramine is being used to treat bile-salt diarrhea, that drug will further reduce the quantity of available bile salts and this will further interfere with fat digestion and, indirectly, with fat absorption. Unabsorbed fat is broken down by bacteria in the colon, producing chemicals that have a laxative effect, possibly aggravating the diarrhea. Fortunately, a relatively small number of patients end up having more than a yard of ileum removed, even when they require a second or third resection.

- *Decreased vitamin B_{12} absorption:* Another function of the ileum is to absorb vitamin B_{12}. If a portion of your ileum is removed, you may have subnormal vitamin B_{12} absorption. If this is the case, no amount of swallowed B_{12} will fix the problem, since there is simply not enough ileum available to absorb it. A few months after the resection, it is a good idea to have a Schilling test, to determine whether B_{12} absorption is normal or not. The test has no risks and is very accurate. But if more than two feet (60 centimeters) of your ileum are removed, B_{12} absorption will not be normal, and there's no point to doing a Schilling test.

  For the Schilling test, you are given an injection of B_{12} and then asked to drink a radioactive B_{12} fluid (don't worry; there's no danger!) Then you collect your urine for two days – in a separate container for each day – and the radioactivity is measured to indicate the amount of B_{12} that your body absorbed.

Some doctors simply put their patients on B_{12} shots after resection of a piece of ileum. However, these injections go on once a month – forever. If you do not go on regular injections, your blood level of B_{12} should be measured intermittently. For some people it is easier and simpler to take the injections, without having the Schilling test. In some countries, you can get a B_{12} product in the form of a nose spray. You may prefer this to monthly injections, but it is expensive, and must be used twice a week. A lack of vitamin B_{12} can cause brain damage, so don't forget about it!

Surgery for Jejunal Crohn's Disease
Most jejunal disease is treated by resection, but some people undergo strictureplasty. The ileum is able to compensate completely for the loss of the jejunum, even with extensive resections, so side effects of jejunal resection are uncommon.

Surgery for Duodenal Crohn's Disease
A few people develop narrowing of the lumen (channel) in the duodenum, so that food cannot pass. Resection or strictureplasty surgery is technically difficult because of the duodenum's anatomic location. Strictureplasty is possible in some cases. When it isn't, a bypass operation called a gastrojejunostomy is done. In this operation, a loop of upper jejunum is surgically attached (anastomosed) to the stomach. Several side effects may occur, but they are beyond the scope of this book.

Surgery for Crohn's Disease of the Stomach
People with Crohn's of the stomach rarely require surgery. If they do, it is mainly because of narrowing and obstruction of

the lower third of the stomach. The usual operation is a gastrojejunostomy, as described above.

Surgery for Crohn's Disease of the Esophagus
Esophageal Crohn's disease is extremely rare. Part or all of the esophagus (swallowing tube) can be removed, if necessary. Some surgeons simply pull the stomach up into the chest and connect it to the remaining esophagus. Others use a section of the patient's jejunum or colon to bridge the gap.

Surgery for Crohn's Disease of the Colon (Crohn's Colitis)
Surgery for Crohn's disease of the colon varies according to how much of the colon is involved, how severe the disease is, what the surgeon and gastroenterologist advise, and what the patient or the patient's family wants. The common reasons for surgery for Crohn's colitis are the same as for Crohn's disease in general: failure of medical therapy to control the disease adequately, abscesses with or without fistulas, and obstructions.

Side Effects of Surgery for Crohn's Colitis
After small segments of the colon are surgically removed, bowel habits should generally be normal. But since the function of the colon is to remove water from the stool, the more colon is lost, the more likely it is that you will have diarrhea. This can often be controlled with antidiarrheal drugs.

Side Effects of Ostomies with the Rectum Left in Place
Some of the stool consists of mucus, living and dead bacteria, and dead lining cells of the bowel. Even if the rectum is disconnected, it continues to produce mucus, provide a home for bacteria, and shed its lining regularly. In other words, it continues to make stool!

Surgery for Crohn's Colitis

Location of disease	Possible operations	Advantages	Disadvantages
Most or all of colon (including rectum)	• Total proctocolectomy & Brooke ileostomy	• Lowest chance of recurrence	• Perineal incision, which may not heal completely
	• Subtotal colectomy, Brooke ileostomy, oversewn rectum	• No perineal incision	• Risk of persistent or recurrent disease in rectum • Access to rectum for cancer checkup may be difficult
Most or all of colon but normal rectum	• Total proctocolectomy & Brooke ileostomy	• Lowest chance of recurrence	• Perineal incision • Need for appliance
	• Subtotal colectomy, Brooke ileostomy, oversewn rectum	• No perineal incision	• Risk of persistent or recurrent disease in rectum • Need for appliance • Access to rectum for cancer checkup may be difficult
	• Subtotal colectomy & ileorectal anastomosis	• No perineal incision • No need for appliance	• Highest chance of recurrent disease in ileum or rectum • Need for cancer surveillance of rectum • Frequent bowel movements

Location of disease	Possible operations	Advantages	Disadvantages
Short segment (excluding rectum)	• Segmental resection	• Low chance of diarrhea • Simple operation	• High chance of recurrent disease
Rectum only	• Colostomy only	• Simple operation	• Need for appliance • Possible persistent or recurrent rectal or peri-anal disease
	• Colostomy and proctectomy	• Better chance of prolonged relief of symptoms	• Perineal incision • Need for appliance
Ileum and colon	• Selective, if symptoms are distinctively ileum *or* colon	• Conserves bowel (fewer side effects)	• Higher recurrence rate

Although there is no food residue, the stool that is made accumulates and must be emptied every so often. Some people make more; others make less. But everyone who has a disconnected rectum will continue to have the urge to have a bowel movement in the normal way every so often. Some patients, particularly those who have not been warned, are confused when they get the urge to go to the toilet. "I must be going crazy. My rectum is disconnected from my intestines but I still feel I have to have a bowel movement!" Of course they're not crazy. They are getting the urge to pass the nonfood portion of the stool.

You shouldn't resist the urge. If you do, the stool will accumulate. Just like normal stool that is held in, it will get drier and drier and harder and harder. It will accumulate until the rectum fills up. When that happens, you will generally start to get increasing pressure and discomfort in the pelvic region. Sooner or later you'll see a doctor, who will examine you and find that the rectum is full. Some patients find it necessary to give themselves a small enema every so often.

Recurring Crohn's Disease after Surgery

The chance of Crohn's disease coming back after surgery is highest if you have combined small-bowel and colon disease, slightly lower if you have pure small-bowel disease, and lowest if you have pure colon disease, provided you have had all of the colon removed, or all of the colon except for the rectum. Just to make things more confusing, there are three different kinds of recurrence referred to in the medical literature. One kind is *endoscopic* recurrence – that is, recurrent disease that is found by examining your bowel with a scope. European researchers have demonstrated that many people undergoing small-bowel resection have evidence of new disease in the ileum visible with the colonoscope within twelve weeks of surgery; however, the vast majority of these patients will not have symptoms at that time. *Clinical recurrence* is what is of concern to most patients – a return of symptoms and signs of the disease. *Surgical recurrence* is defined as the need for further surgery. Despite numerous studies, we have little knowledge about the factors that influence clinically recurrent Crohn's disease. Recent evidence has suggested that smoking increases the risk, and stopping smoking decreases it.

For individuals with pure small-bowel disease or those with combined small-bowel and large-bowel disease, most recurrences will be in the ileum, starting from the anastomosis (connection) and extending upward. Why it is much less common for the disease to recur downstream from the anastomosis is just one more mystery of Crohn's disease. The symptoms, signs, and extent of disease prior to surgery cannot be used to predict the symptoms, signs, and extent when the disease comes back.

Current figures suggest that about 15 to 25 percent of patients with small-bowel disease (with or without colonic disease) will have symptoms of the disease within two years of surgery, 30 to 50 percent within about five years, and about 70 percent within ten years. It is believed that, if people lived long enough, the recurrence rate of small-bowel Crohn's would be 100 percent.

For disease of the colon the situation is not so clear. If a short segment of diseased colon is removed, there is probably a 75 percent chance of developing further disease. But if the entire colon plus rectum is removed, some centers suggest that the recurrence rate in the ileum will be as low as 10 percent, while other equally authoritative centers suggest that the risk is as high as 40 percent. There is also a higher risk of recurrent Crohn's disease in the ileum in people who undergo subtotal colectomy and ileorectal anastomosis than in those with subtotal colectomy and ileostomy. On the other hand, the chance that someone will need removal of the rectum (proctectomy) is higher in people who have had an ileostomy (60 percent in ten years) than in those with an ileorectal anastomosis (20 percent). This is probably because those with an ileostomy are more likely to have had significant rectal disease before surgery.

Can Someone with Crohn's Disease Have a Pelvic-Pouch Operation?
Some doctors feel that this is an option for selected patients with Crohn's in the colon only. It seems important that such people have no history, past or present, of small-bowel Crohn's, or of anal involvement.

One of the reasons the statistics on surgery for Crohn's colitis are so confusing is that far fewer patients require surgery, compared with people who have Crohn's disease of the ileum, or ileum and colon. So in any given center for IBD there may not be enough patients to provide statistically meaningful numbers about the outcome of a particular operation.

Looking at Crohn's disease overall, without regard to where the disease occurs, various studies have suggested that the chance of needing any surgery for Crohn's disease is about 80 percent. The chance of needing a second operation after a first resection is 25 to 40 percent at five years, 30 to 60 percent at ten years, and 40 to 70 percent at twenty years.

Laparoscopic Surgery for Ulcerative Colitis and Crohn's Disease
Recent reports indicate that all standard operations for IBD can be performed using laparoscopic techniques. However, the surgeon's prior experience with these techniques is important, particularly when dealing with ill patients or complications.

Just because an operation can be done this way doesn't mean it's the best way for everyone. Some complex cases are better managed with laparoscopic-assisted surgery; this means that one incision (and one scar) will be larger than the others, but not as large as the typical scar from open surgery. This technique is generally chosen to shorten the length of an operation. Other advantages of laparoscopic surgery include less pain after surgery, less time in hospital, and more rapid recovery. The cosmetic result – much smaller scars – is particularly valuable for children and young adults.

Short-Bowel Syndrome
As we've said, many people with small-bowel Crohn's disease require more than one operation. A small number will end up with not enough bowel surface area to allow normal digestion and absorption of nutrients. This is known as *short-bowel syndrome*. Some of these people can cope with a restricted diet and the use of specialized products such as MCT oil; some will need home TPN (see Chapter 5).

Small-Bowel Transplantation
This form of treatment is still in its early stages. While it is sometimes successful, its use is generally restricted to people who

> Laparoscopic surgery is popularly known as keyhole surgery because the surgeon gets into the patient's abdomen through a series of "keyhole" incisions – little cuts through the abdominal wall. Carbon dioxide gas (which is safe) is pumped into the abdomen to create some space between the organs, allowing the surgeon to see what he or she is doing. Various instruments are placed through these incisions, and an operation is performed with the aid of a television video system.

must come off home TPN because of advanced liver disease, recurrent blood clots in major veins, or a lack of adequate veins for administration of the TPN, because of previous clots and/or infection, resulting in scarring and blockage of the veins.

Surgical Treatment for Abscesses and Fistulas

About 25 percent of people with Crohn's disease are troubled by peri-anal disease, which literally means disease around the anus. The problems that usually require surgery include abscesses (boils) and fistulas (see Chapter 9).

How Does an Abscess Form?

Abscesses and fistulas in Crohn's disease arise because of little breaks in the inner lining of the small or large intestine. These breaks in the lining allow germs (such as bacteria) that are normally present in the intestine to get into tissues such as the mesentery or the tissues around the rectum, where they shouldn't be. This is referred to as a "confined perforation." The presence of the germs triggers a response by the body that is just like a country responding to an invading force. The body sends in white blood cells (the army) to attack the bacteria. The white cells kill some bacteria and the bacteria kill some white cells. Initially, the white cells win. However, once the break in the lining lets germs exit from the small bowel or colon, it almost always stays open. The result is that bacteria continue to enter the tissues, and this leads to a continuing

How an Abscess Forms in Crohn's Disease

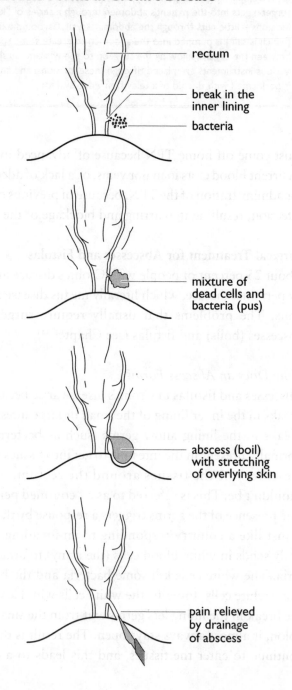

rectum

break in the
inner lining

bacteria

mixture of
dead cells and
bacteria (pus)

abscess (boil)
with stretching
of overlying skin

pain relieved
by drainage
of abscess

infection, a continuing response by the body, and a continuing presence of white blood cells. The result is the gradual accumulation of pus, which is a mixture of living and dead white cells and living and dead germs. Common examples of pus in everyday life are the yellow or green stuff that comes out of your nose when you have a bad cold or the greenish yellow substance that appears on the surface of your skin a few days after you suffer a bad scrape.

When you initially have an abscess, you don't feel anything. But gradually the accumulating pus puts pressure on the adjacent tissues. Sooner or later, the infection results in swelling and pain, and possibly a fever as well.

How Is an Abscess Treated?

The treatment for a collection of pus is to drain it. Sometimes the body will cause the drainage to occur without a doctor having to do anything. Think of having an acne pimple on your forehead. As the pimple grows, it becomes more and more uncomfortable because the skin around the pimple is being stretched due to the pressure of the pus within it. Many people with a painful acne pimple will squeeze it because they know that this will pop a little hole in the surface of the skin, most of the pus will drain out, and the pain will go away. A somewhat more pleasant way of accomplishing the same thing is to apply warm wet compresses to the area. This will soften the skin and make it easier for the pimple to spring a leak and drain itself.

An abdominal or peri-anal abscess is really just like a giant pimple. If the abscess bulges toward the surface of the abdomen or buttock, it may drain spontaneously. If you soak the area (by taking sitz baths, if it is a peri-anal abscess) this will encourage drainage. The skin in the area of the abscess softens and the pressure inside the abscess may cause it to break open and drain.

Unfortunately, an abscess must often become quite large before it bulges the surface of the skin, and this means that it

What Is a Fistula?

A fistula is an abnormal connection between a hollow structure (such as the rectum) and the skin surface or between two hollow structures such as two loops of bowel, or bowel and bladder, or bowel and vagina. The path that the fistula follows is referred to as a "fistulous tract," and may be short or quite long.

Peri-anal Fistula

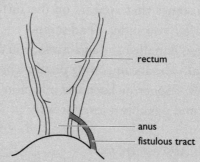

- rectum
- anus
- fistulous tract

Recto-vaginal Fistula

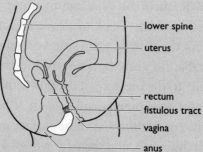

- lower spine
- uterus
- rectum
- fistulous tract
- vagina
- anus

Ileo-vesical (Ileum-to-bladder) Fistula

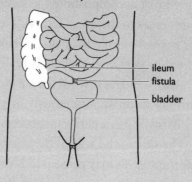

- ileum
- fistula
- bladder

can become quite painful. Many people cannot tolerate the pain while waiting for an abscess to drain spontaneously. Indeed, they should not wait – occasionally people become quite ill. At a hospital or doctor's office the abscess can be drained by freezing the area and making a small hole with a scalpel or a needle through the skin directly into the abscess. If a peri-anal abscess is large, you may have to be taken to the operating room and given a general anesthetic so a surgeon can adequately drain it. Large abdominal abscesses are almost always easily drained with the aid of ultrasound or CAT scan guidance.

Draining the abscess does not always end the problem in people with Crohn's disease. In most cases, the little opening in the inner lining of the intestine that led to the abscess remains, as we've said. After drainage of the abscess, the result is a connection between the inside of the intestine and the outside world via the skin. This is one example of a fistula.

If a peri-anal abscess does not point toward the skin but points and presses instead on the patient's bladder, it may drain spontaneously into the bladder. This will solve the immediate problem of the abscess, but the person will be left with a fistula to the bladder that will require treatment. The same situation can occur if the abscess points toward and pushes on the vagina. If a fistula to the bladder, vagina, or skin surface in a location other than the perineum is treated surgically, removal of the piece of intestine that is the source of the fistula is usually necessary. Some fistulas simply connect two segments of intestine; often nothing needs to be done about these.

Sometimes multiple breaks in the lining occur close together. This may result in a large mass of inflamed tissue containing many little abscesses, called a *phlegmon*. Treatment for this condition is almost always surgical resection of the segment of intestine that is the source of infection.

Fistulous Tract with Chronic Abscess

i

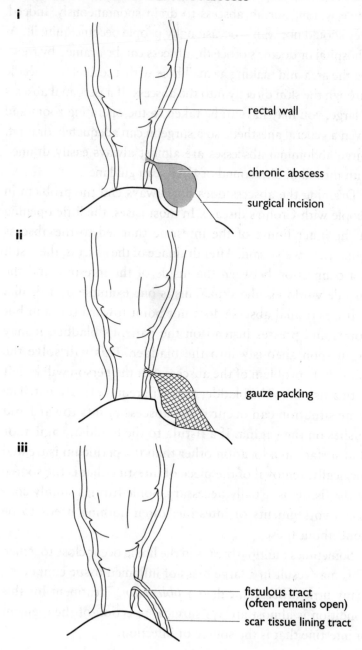

rectal wall

chronic abscess

surgical incision

ii

gauze packing

iii

fistulous tract
(often remains open)

scar tissue lining tract

Treatment of a Chronic Abscess

Many people with peri-anal abscesses can be treated with sitz baths and antibiotics, but some need surgery. In some cases the surgeon must create a wedge-shaped opening into the abscess to clean it out thoroughly. Afterward, the wound cavity may be packed with gauze, which is usually changed daily. If this is not done, the wound usually closes over at the surface faster than it does deeper down, so that the abscess cavity remains and becomes filled with pus again. The packing keeps the skin wound open so that the wound heals from the bottom up (or, to put it another way, from the inside out).

If the procedure is totally successful, the area heals completely, leaving a scar. However, in most cases the patient is left with a fistulous tract, which is a narrow, straight, tubelike path from the inside of the bowel out to the skin, without an abscess cavity. Drainage is usually a relatively minor problem and most people can put up with it.

Unfortunately, those people who develop peri-anal fistulas often get other abscesses and fistulas and need surgery again.

Adhesions

Any time a patient has surgery on the GI tract, bands of scar tissue are going to develop afterward. These bands, known as adhesions, will run from the point of surgery to other segments of intestine, to other organs, or to the peritoneum (lining of the abdominal cavity), particularly at the site of the previous incision. In most people they do not cause any problems. Adhesions don't hurt. What they can do is fix the intestine at a certain point so that, if it becomes twisted, an obstruction will occur. Most such obstructions get better without surgical treatment. However, some people need surgery to untwist the bowel and cut the adhesions. Of course, new adhesions will form, but usually they will not cause trouble.

E I G H T

Children with IBD

Both ulcerative colitis and Crohn's disease can begin at any age. However, ulcerative colitis is rare in infancy, while Crohn's disease is not unusual. Fifteen percent of people with ulcerative colitis develop it before the age of twenty, whereas in Crohn's disease the figure is 25 to 30 percent.

Research has suggested that second-hand smoke increases the risk of inflammatory bowel disease, particularly Crohn's disease, in children. One study showed a possible increased risk of ulcerative colitis as well, even though smoking seems to protect against ulcerative colitis in adults (see Chapter 2).

Diagnosing IBD in Children

Many aspects of ulcerative colitis and Crohn's disease in children are identical to those in adults, but there are some important differences. The symptoms of both diseases seem to be more pronounced in children than in adults. There is also some evidence that children have more intestinal complications (see Chapter 9). However, they have fewer nonintestinal problems than adults.

Most children with ulcerative colitis are diagnosed fairly promptly, because blood is found in the stool. The diagnosis

of Crohn's disease, however, is often delayed. Previc
time between the onset of symptoms and a diagnosis o. ......
averaged three years. This has decreased in the past twenty-
five years because of greater awareness of the disease.

Many children with Crohn's develop the typical crampy
abdominal pain, diarrhea, and weight loss, but some have only
a low-grade fever with few other symptoms. Sometimes it's
hard to tell what's going on. Many otherwise normal young
children suffer from abdominal pain related to lactose intolerance or constipation, and some children complain about
abdominal pain that is a result of emotional stress. Poor
appetite and weight loss can lead to an erroneous diagnosis of
anorexia nervosa. In some children, the only sign of Crohn's
initially is a failure to grow; parents and doctors are alerted
by the child's small size or delayed puberty.

The Issue of Growth

Even after an accurate diagnosis is made, growth failure in children with IBD is a concern. However, we've learned a lot in
the past 25 years. We used to think that using glucocorticoids
to treat the disease was a major factor in delayed growth. The
bulk of the evidence now suggests that the major factor is how
active the disease is. The more severe the disease, and the longer
the time it is active, the more growth will be delayed, even prevented. Glucocorticoids may play some role in delayed growth,
but growth is likely to improve if the drugs suppress the disease
so the child will eat better.

Drug Therapy for Children with IBD

Generally children receive the same drugs as adults, but the
doses of some need to be adjusted to body weight, and a few
drugs are avoided because they can interfere with the development of certain tissues. Because IBD is more aggressive in

children, steroids are given more frequently to them than to adults. As with adults, the immunosuppressive drugs azathioprine and 6-mercaptopurine are currently considered the best long-term strategy for children who can't get off steroids, need frequent steroids, or need to avoid steroids.

Extra Nutrition for Children with Crohn's

Canadian researchers have been leaders in demonstrating that some children with Crohn's disease will grow more if their normal diet is supplemented with nightly feeds of a liquid diet (see Chapter 5). In fact, many children learn to slip small feeding tubes through their noses down into their stomachs each night at bedtime. A bag of enteral (sterilized liquid) diet is hung on a pole and dripped into the tube while the child is asleep. In the morning, the child pulls out the tube and has a normal day. A thousand or more extra kilocalories (4,184 kilojoules) can be taken in this way.

Surgery for Children with IBD

Obviously, the most effective way to reduce inflammation is to remove it surgically. Indeed, doctors tend to be somewhat more aggressive about treating children surgically, because of the concern about growth, and also because the IBD tends to be more aggressive. Nevertheless, unless puberty has already begun, there is a span of several years in which to suppress the disease and allow growth. No one should jump to the conclusion that children should immediately undergo surgery because their growth is delayed. Not all children with IBD will grow simply because they have surgery; they may just be naturally short. Laparoscopic surgery is particularly attractive, because the scars are much smaller and less noticeable.

Psychological Effects of IBD on Children

Children – particularly teenagers – are very anxious n(
seen as different from their peers; their self-consciousness,
and the intolerance of other children, often leads to a degree
of isolation. Adjustment to an ostomy is particularly difficult;
having a "buddy" (another child of similar age who has already
adjusted to an ostomy) can help. If a child isn't available, a
young adult is next best. You can ask your medical/surgical
team to find a buddy for you. Many centers have an IBD
patient database, which is helpful.

Most children, like most adults, become tough as a result
of having a chronic disease. But this takes time. Parents must
try to treat these children the same way they treat their other
children. Whenever possible, children with IBD should be
allowed to participate in normal activities. Unnecessary dietary
restrictions should be avoided. For example, there is no evidence that people with IBD need to avoid "junk foods."

It is natural to feel depressed when IBD is diagnosed or
when it flares up. Many kids think, "Why me?" However,
once treatment begins and the symptoms subside, most will
perk up. During a flare-up, extra rest *may* be necessary. When
improvement comes, regular activities *may* have to be resumed
gradually.

It is desirable for the child to establish a comfortable relationship with the doctor. Family, close friends, and, at times,
other patients can be a big help, but the doctor-patient relationship remains extremely important.

N I N E

Complications
of IBD

omplications are unforeseen conditions that occur during the course of a disease. Sometimes they arise before the disease is diagnosed, and serve as symptoms or signs that lead a physician to the disease.

The complications of IBD can be divided into two types: those related to the intestine itself, and those outside the intestine. Here are some of the more common ones.

Complications in the Intestine

Toxic Megacolon

From a medical viewpoint the most severe complication of any type of colitis is toxic megacolon. The word "toxic" means that the patient is acutely ill with fever, abdominal pain, loss of appetite, diarrhea, nausea, and possibly vomiting. "Megacolon" refers to the fact that part or all of the colon is abnormally wide in diameter.

In this condition, the muscular wall of the colon becomes more or less paralyzed. As a result, the gas normally produced by the bacteria in the colon accumulates instead of passing out the rectum. Toxic megacolon is the most feared complication of colitis mainly because it is sometimes associated with perforations (holes) in the wall of the colon. The contents of the bowel (including bacteria) can leak into the abdominal cavity, resulting in *peritonitis*, a condition in which the lining of the abdominal wall is inflamed. This is a very serious, sometimes fatal illness. The perforations require emergency surgery. The usual operation is subtotal colectomy, Brooke ileostomy, and mucous fistula of the rectum (see Chapter 7).

If there is no evidence of perforation, standard treatment is steroids, but surgery is often necessary.

Toxic megacolon can occur with both ulcerative colitis and Crohn's disease of the colon. It is less common in Crohn's colitis because, as the disease progresses, the colon wall becomes thick, scarred, and less likely to stretch. Toxic megacolon is more common in people who have extensive colitis than it is with colitis limited to a relatively small segment of the colon.

Toxic colitis is similar to toxic megacolon; the main difference is that the colon diameter is still normal. The treatment is the same.

Strictures

Both ulcerative colitis and Crohn's disease can be complicated by strictures, or localized areas of narrowing. Strictures are much more common in Crohn's disease than in ulcerative colitis, because Crohn's causes inflammation of the full thickness of the wall of the bowel. Ulcerative colitis generally involves only the inner lining.

Strictures may lead to bowel obstruction, which may be temporary (acute) or permanent (chronic). Bowel obstruction is the most common complication of small-bowel Crohn's disease. It can occur suddenly or gradually. Sudden or acute obstruction

ually associated with crampy abdominal pain, nausea, and metimes vomiting. You may have increased diarrhea, or you may stop passing stool, and even gas, completely. Acute obstruction is not a complication of either ulcerative or Crohn's colitis.

If you have chronic obstruction, which is partial, you will experience abdominal pain, nausea, and bloating of the abdomen after meals. The interval between the meal and the symptoms depends on the site of blockage. Less than one hour suggests small bowel; more than one hour suggests colon.

Perforations, Abscesses, and Fistulas

Perforations can occur in both ulcerative colitis and Crohn's disease. Abscesses and fistulas are complications of Crohn's disease only.

Perforations are holes that develop in the wall of any hollow structure. As a result the bowel contents (including bacteria) leak into the abdominal cavity. If a perforation develops rapidly, the intestinal contents will spill into the peritoneal cavity and cause peritonitis. This is called a "free" perforation. The vast majority of free perforations in ulcerative colitis occur with toxic megacolon (see above). Free perforations can also occur in attacks of severe colitis without megacolon (i.e., toxic colitis), but such events are rare. Free perforations are also rare in Crohn's disease, except with toxic megacolon. The treatment in both ulcerative colitis and Crohn's disease is emergency surgery.

If a perforation develops slowly, the body usually reacts by "walling off" the hole in the bowel wall so that peritonitis does not result. This is called a "confined" perforation and results in the formation of an abscess (popularly called a "boil"). An abscess is a walled-off collection of pus. As explained earlier, pus is a mixture of live and dead bacteria and live and dead white blood cells, with or without living and dead cells from adjacent tissues. An abscess can be virtually any size, from tiny and visible only under a microscope to something the size of a golfball, or larger.

A fistula, as we've seen, is an abnormal connection between two hollow structures (such as bowel and bladder or bowel and vagina) or between a hollow structure and the skin. Once a fistula has been created, by the burrowing nature of the inflammation in Crohn's disease or by drainage (spontaneous or surgical) of an abscess, it is likely to drain intermittently or constantly. Antibiotics are often helpful. If the problem persists, surgery may be necessary.

Peri-anal Disease
Strictly speaking, this term refers to disease around the anus. But from a practical point of view it includes disease within the anal canal, as well as around it.

Hemorrhoids
Any condition that causes diarrhea or constipation is likely to lead to enlargement of the veins within the anal canal. The enlarged veins are known as hemorrhoids, or "piles." They are often felt as soft bumps protruding from the anal canal or immediately around it. Uncomplicated hemorrhoids don't hurt.

Occasionally a hemorrhoid becomes blocked by a blood clot. This is called a "thrombosed hemorrhoid." It causes considerable pain in the region of the anus, and the sufferer will likely be unwilling – or even unable – to sit. The pain is relieved dramatically if the hemorrhoid ruptures or if a surgeon makes a small cut in it to relieve the tension in the vein wall and surrounding tissues.

Skin Tags

When hemorrhoids bulge, they stretch the overlying skin. When the hemorrhoids shrink, the stretched skin remains and is commonly referred to as a "skin tag." In Crohn's disease, but not in ulcerative colitis, these tags can become swollen and firm. Once tags thicken, they usually stay that way. They don't hurt, but they can be annoying, especially because bits of stool can get trapped between them and this can lead to chronic irritation of the skin and itching. In most people with Crohn's disease, it is best to avoid surgical removal of these swollen tags.

Anal Fissures

Many people with hemorrhoids also develop anal fissures. An anal fissure is a cut or tear in the skin of the anal canal. This skin is extremely sensitive, so fissures can be quite painful, especially during a bowel movement and shortly after. The pain is often felt as a stretching or tearing during a bowel movement and as a burning afterward. People with Crohn's disease sometimes get fissures that are wider, longer, and deeper than those that occur in ulcerative colitis. When a fissure becomes deep, it becomes covered with a layer of pus and may be referred to as an "anal ulcer."

Abscesses and Fistulas

Many people with Crohn's disease develop abscesses and fistulas in and around the anus. A detailed discussion of how these develop and how they are treated appears in Chapter 7.

Strictures of the Anal Canal

These are common in Crohn's disease, but sometimes occur with ulcerative colitis as well. If your stools are very loose, you will be unaware of the narrowing. When stools are formed, the diameter of the stool is restricted by the diameter of the stricture. People with strictures have narrow stools, but many people with narrow stools don't have strictures! The simple act of straining to have a bowel movement prevents the anal sphincter from relaxing properly, and this forces the stool to be squeezed out through a narrower passage.

Mild anal strictures need no treatment. More severe strictures may require periodic stretching. This can be done manually with the doctor's gloved finger or with instruments known as dilators.

Iron-Deficiency Anemia, Hemorrhage, and Massive Hemorrhage

"Anemia" means that the blood contains a reduced number of circulating red blood cells. It can be due to a deficiency of iron, folate (a B vitamin), or vitamin B_{12}. But even when these nutrients are present in adequate amounts, some people are anemic simply as a result of having a chronic disease. Chronic inflammation in the body suppresses the blood-producing activity of the bone marrow (see "erythropoietin" in Chapter 6).

Folate deficiency can occur if you are taking sulfasalazine (see Chapter 6) or you are severely malnourished. Vitamin B_{12} deficiency may occur if you have extensive ileal disease, or after surgical removal of the ileum (see Chapter 7). Iron deficiency, however, is a little more complicated.

Anemia due to iron deficiency can develop in one of three ways. You may not be getting enough iron in your diet; this is uncommon but possible, especially if you eat little red meat or organ meats such as liver. Even if you have enough iron in your diet, you may not be absorbing it for some reason. Iron absorption is commonly decreased in people with celiac disease, which is especially common in individuals of Irish descent. If you consume and absorb enough iron but still have iron deficiency, the only other possibility is that you are losing more iron than you are taking in. The way we lose iron is by losing blood. You can lose up to an ounce and a half (40 milliliters) of blood a day in the stool without seeing anything, if the bleeding comes from high enough up in the GI tract that the blood is thoroughly mixed in with the stool. Losing small amounts of blood on a daily basis will lead to iron-deficiency anemia over a period of several months.

Anemia in Ulcerative Colitis

No one with a recent onset of ulcerative colitis should have iron-deficiency anemia simply due to the colitis. Even though there is obviously blood in the stool, the amount is almost always less than you think; it takes very little bright red fluid to color a whole bowl of toilet water red! Unless bleeding is truly heavy, the bone marrow is able to use available stores of iron to keep the red-blood-cell count in the normal range. If you have had several attacks of ulcerative colitis, however, you will likely require some iron supplementation, since the stores of iron within the body eventually get used up.

Occasionally the bleeding is heavier than average and anemia may develop before the body has a chance to respond and produce new red blood cells.

Anemia in Crohn's Disease

Even in the absence of visible bleeding, people with Crohn's disease frequently develop iron-deficiency anemia. There are usually multiple ulcers (open sores) in the small or large intestine, and chronic, continuous, low-grade blood loss is common.

Sudden episodes of visible bleeding can occur, but not often. This happens when an ulcer burrows into a large blood vessel, generally an artery. Fortunately, the normal repair mechanisms of the body usually seal off the bleeding vessel. In some people sudden bleeding of this type occurs only once, but in others it recurs or becomes persistent, and may require surgical treatment.

If people with extensive disease in the ileum or an extensive ileal resection are not given vitamin B_{12}, they may eventually develop anemia, because they may be less able to absorb vitamin B_{12}. The need for B_{12} can be determined with a Schilling test (see Chapter 7).

Massive Hemorrhage
Rarely in Crohn's disease, and very rarely in ulcerative colitis, sudden and massive bleeding occurs. In Crohn's disease, sudden massive bleeding may start in someone who is otherwise feeling well, or during an attack. In most cases the source of such bleeding is the colon. Emergency surgery removes the colon. If the source of bleeding is the small intestine, the diseased segment will likely have to be removed. Even if bleeding stops spontaneously, the occurrence of a life-threatening hemorrhage usually necessitates removing the diseased bowel to avoid another, possibly fatal hemorrhage.

Recent studies have shown that the drugs azathioprine and infliximab can heal Crohn's disease in some people. If you have had a hemorrhage, your doctor may decide to try to heal your disease instead of advising you to have an operation. The risks and benefits must be carefully considered.

In ulcerative colitis, massive hemorrhage generally happens during a severe attack. Here the inflammatory process goes more deeply into the intestinal wall than usual and disrupts larger blood vessels. Surgical removal of the colon is often necessary.

Complications Outside the Intestine

Inflammatory bowel disease is associated with numerous complications outside the intestines. The areas commonly involved include the joints, the skin, the mouth, the liver, the bile duct, the kidneys, the blood, and the eyes.

Painful Joints

Ten to 20 percent of people with IBD have joint pains at some time. Joint disease associated with intestinal disease is referred to as *enteropathic arthropathy. Arthralgia* means joint pain. *Arthritis* refers to joints that are inflamed. A person with arthritis also has arthralgia, but many people with arthralgia do not have arthritis. I make this distinction because patients with joint pains often say that they have arthritis, but notice that their doctor does not use that term. From the patient's point of view, the terminology may not matter very much.

Arthritis associated with IBD is nondestructive: that is, the inflamed joints are not permanently damaged, as they are in rheumatoid or gouty arthritis, for example. You may have a lot of pain and swelling, but it is temporary, with no long-lasting effects.

Typically, arthritis of IBD occurs mainly in the large joints (e.g., knees, ankles) and tends to move from one joint to another. It may flare up when the IBD flares up, and settle down when the IBD settles down. However, it can precede any bowel symptoms by several years and can flare up when the bowel disease is relatively quiet. If the inflamed bowel is surgically removed, this form of arthritis goes away. Of course, if the disease is Crohn's disease and it recurs, then the arthritis may recur.

Ankylosing Spondylitis (AS or Sacroiliitis)

This is a type of arthritis involving the sacroiliac joints, with or without involvement of the joints of the spine. You may have pain or stiffness in the lower back, though such symptoms are more often due to ordinary spinal-disc disease. If the disease is looked for with X-rays and other tests, it is found in many people who do not have symptoms. As with arthritis, this condition can precede the onset of bowel symptoms by several years. Unlike arthritis, the symptoms of ankylosing spondylitis do not correlate at all with bowel disease activity, and do not improve after surgery on the bowel. The drug infliximab is useful in some cases.

Ankylosing spondylitis can also occur independently of IBD, and is indistinguishable from AS in people with IBD. AS occurs in association with ulcerative colitis much more than with Crohn's disease.

Bone Disease

Osteonecrosis
This term literally means "bone death." It was previously thought that osteonecrosis in people with IBD was always a complication of steroid therapy. Recently, however, it was reported in two IBD patients who had never received steroids. The two most typical locations are the hips and the knees. This condition is extremely uncommon, but it can cause considerable disability. It leads to damage (known as avascular necrosis) of the hip or knee joints and usually requires artificial total hip or knee replacement.

Osteoporosis (Soft Bones)
People with IBD frequently have osteoporosis. This is often blamed solely on steroid therapy, but is more likely related to a combination of factors, including low calcium intake, lack of exercise, steroid use, and possibly an inherited tendency to develop osteoporosis. In recent years, with the advent of a test

as bone densitometry, monitoring of bone health has ne considerably more accurate. This test involves a imal amount of radiation. It is brief (about twenty minutes), painless, and safe. Prior to this diagnostic technique, we had to rely on bone X-rays, which do not reveal evidence of osteoporosis until it is far advanced, or bone biopsy (removing a sample of bone), which is not practical for screening large numbers of patients.

Both calcium and vitamin D are necessary to form bone. As we saw in Chapter 5, vitamin D is available in food and vitamin supplements, and is also produced in the body when the skin is exposed to sunlight. People with Crohn's disease who have had more than a yard (about a meter) of ileum removed may not be able to absorb enough vitamin D and, possibly, calcium. They may be particularly susceptible to osteoporosis. The risk increases in postmenopausal women. In some people, measuring blood levels of vitamin D is helpful. But vitamin D levels can vary considerably with the seasons, because we are exposed to so much less sunlight during the winter months. There are now several drugs for the treatment of osteoporosis.

Sores in the Mouth

About 5 to 10 percent of people with IBD experience intermittent sores in the mouth. These are sometimes indistinguishable from the canker sores (also known as aphthous ulcers) that occur in the general population, but the latter typically occur one at a time, last a few days, and go away. Canker sores in IBD patients often occur in clusters, may be unusually large, and may persist for many days, even a few weeks. These sores usually occur when bowel disease is more active.

In addition to ordinary canker sores, people with Crohn's disease can develop mouth or throat ulcerations that look like Crohn's ulcers in the bowel. Biopsies of these ulcers show micro-

> ## Treating Canker Sores in the Mouth
>
> A treatment proven to be of some value in treating canker sores in the mouth is as follows. You need capsules (250 milligrams each) of the antibiotic tetracycline. Dissolve the contents of one capsule into one or two teaspoons (5 to 10 milliliters) of warm water. Hold the solution in your mouth for ten to fifteen minutes (if you can do it for that long!) and then spit it out. Try to do this four times a day. You should begin this treatment right at the onset of any fresh sores, and continue it for a few days. This can shorten the duration of the sores. Apply the local anesthetic viscous lidocaine directly onto the sores with a Q-Tip just before meals to decrease discomfort during eating.

scopic changes typical of Crohn's disease. Steroids may be needed; there isn't a more specific therapy. Fortunately, these ulcers resolve themselves over a week or two in most patients.

Recent studies show that people with symptomatic Crohn's disease also have more gum infections and cavities than those whose disease is not causing any symptoms. This may simply be due to a difference in diet; some people with Crohn's disease eat an unusually large amount of refined sugars, to replace energy lost by avoidance of other foods.

Skin Diseases

The most common skin abnormality in IBD is *erythema nodosum*. It occurs in 2 to 10 percent of people with IBD, and is somewhat more common in women. It consists of painful, tender red bumps that appear most often on the shins but sometimes show up on other parts of the legs, or even on the arms. It is often associated with a flare-up of IBD, and usually improves as the bowel disease is treated and improves.

Pyoderma gangrenosum (PG) occurs in 1 to 5 percent of people with IBD, and is more common in ulcerative colitis. Most people with PG have extensive colitis. PG begins with a raised, red, tender area of skin which then takes on the appearance of a blister. The roof of the blister breaks down and the result is a skin ulcer. PG usually occurs in multiple locations more or less simultaneously, and the ulcers can be any size, from tiny to extensive. Although these sores are generally painless, they are very unsightly and unpleasant to deal with, and some patients require extensive dressings. The drug infliximab may help.

Diseases of the Liver and Biliary Tract

Fatty liver
Fatty liver is a common complication in IBD. The cause is unknown, but in most cases it is likely malnutrition. Most patients have no symptoms or signs of the condition, it is not serious, and it is usually temporary. However, there are several other causes, so some tests may be needed.

Primary Sclerosing Cholangitis (PSC)
This is one of the most serious complications of IBD. It occurs in 1 to 4 percent of patients, more in people with ulcerative colitis than in those with Crohn's disease. Some people with this condition do not have IBD, but about 70 percent do. "Primary" is a medical way of saying that the cause of the condition is unknown.

"Sclerosing" means "hardening." This disease causes scarring in the biliary tree along with inflammation of the bile duct and/or its branches. The scarring is patchy. It can be present only in the bile duct outside the liver, only in the branches of the biliary tree within the liver, or in both locations.

It is now accepted that there are two types of this disease: small-duct PSC and large-duct PSC. The small-duct form is much less of a problem; it doesn't usually shorten a person's life, cause serious liver damage, or progress to large-duct disease and liver transplantation.

Sclerosing Cholangitis

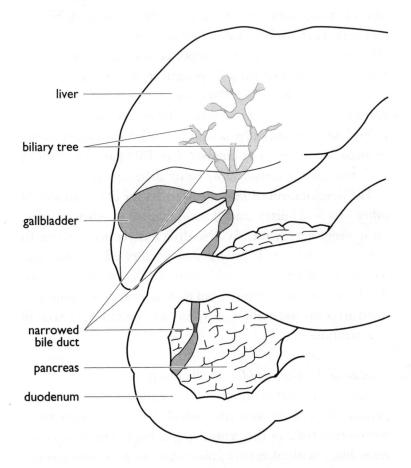

liver

biliary tree

gallbladder

narrowed
bile duct

pancreas

duodenum

PSC can be diagnosed by MRI; the technique is known as an MRCP. But a more exact evaluation requires an ERCP – endoscopic retrograde cholangio-pancreatography – which involves injecting dye into the bile duct. In the small-duct form, these test results will be normal, and a liver biopsy will generally be done to confirm the diagnosis.

Until the 1980s, no satisfactory treatment, medical or surgical, existed for PSC. Patients died of infection in the liver or of complications of liver damage that eventually results from untreated PSC. In the 1980s, cyclosporine was introduced to the field of transplantation. This drug alone was responsible for moving liver transplants from the back pages of newspapers to the front pages. Because of cyclosporine, the success rate in liver transplants increased from 20 percent to 80 percent or more.

Thus, since the mid-1980s, the treatment of choice for patients with *advanced* sclerosing cholangitis has been a liver transplant. Even so, patients with PSC still have a significantly reduced life expectancy compared to IBD patients without PSC, though it is considerably better than it used to be.

The development of new medications for the treatment of other liver and biliary-tract diseases has led to renewed interest in drug therapy for PSC. No drug has yet been proven to arrest or even slow its progression. Studies using a bile acid named *ursodeoxycholic acid* (urso, or UDCA) have shown that liver blood tests improve but there is no apparent improvement in the disease itself. Researchers are continuing to explore new treatments.

Cancer of the Gallbladder or Bile Ducts
Cancer of the gallbladder or bile ducts occurs in about 1 percent of patients with IBD, which is ten to twenty times more often than in the general population. The tumors are more likely with ulcerative colitis than with Crohn's disease.

Gallstones
Bile salts are chemicals produced by the liver. They pass down from the liver into the duodenum dissolved in bile, and help to digest and absorb fat. Cholesterol is also dissolved in bile. People who have extensive disease in the ileum or have had some of the ileum surgically removed absorb and recycle a

smaller percentage of the daily bile-salt output. Since one of the functions of bile salts is to keep the cholesterol in bile dissolved, the reduced level of bile salts allows more cholesterol to come out of solution and form stones in the gallbladder. This applies to those with Crohn's disease only. At the present time, no effort is made to try to prevent these stones from developing. However, many gallstones never cause any symptoms and never require any treatment.

Kidney Diseases
Kidney Stones
Kidney stones, usually composed of either calcium oxalate or uric acid, are much more common in people with IBD than they are in the general population. Most of the increased frequency is in people who have had surgery with removal of bowel.

How Can Kidney Stones Be Prevented?
As with many conditions, prevention is most desirable, if possible. If someone who has had a resection of some kind has looser stools than normal, increasing oral fluid intake and reducing fluid loss in the stool is a good idea. Ileostomy patients are generally advised to consume at least two quarts (about two liters) of fluid a day. However, this is not always possible. Using an antidiarrheal drug such as loperamide or diphenoxylate (see Chapter 6) can be very effective in reducing fluid losses in the stool. Some physicians routinely prescribe low-oxalate diets for patients who have had an extensive ileal resection and/or those with extensive ileal disease, to reduce the risk of calcium oxalate stones.

What If Stones Are Already Present?
Most stones will pass through the urinary tract spontaneously. Stones stuck within a ureter often need to be treated by a urologist, a specialist in diseases of the urinary system. Stones that

remain in the kidney are sometimes not treated but are monitored with ultrasound. The pain of kidney stones is not always typical. It is usually in the back, but sometimes it is felt in the abdomen, particularly below the waist on one side or the other. This may initially make you and your doctor think that the pain is due to the IBD. If the pain is not like your usual pain, consider the possibility of a kidney stone.

Hydronephrosis
This literally means "water kidney." If a ureter is blocked, the back-pressure on the kidney from the excess urine that cannot pass will cause the urine-collecting system to become stretched. If this persists, the pressure on the kidney can permanently damage it. Most cases occur in people with Crohn's ileitis, due to pressure on the lower end of the right ureter from the inflammatory process. Hydronephrosis is easily diagnosed with ultrasound, and mild cases may improve without surgery.

Amyloidosis
This rare disease causes widespread protein deposits in organs and tissues throughout the body. These deposits damage or destroy cells and interfere with organ function. Amyloidosis can occur in people who have no other disease, as well as in association with a variety of chronic diseases.

When it comes to IBD, amyloidosis occurs mainly with Crohn's disease, and only rarely in people with ulcerative colitis. It has been found in up to 25 percent of Crohn's patients studied at autopsy, but is found in only about 1 percent of living patients – and in many of these people, it is not causing any problems. However, when amyloidosis does cause serious illness, it is generally because it involves the kidneys, with kidney failure as an eventual result. Some experts think that amyloidosis can stabilize or even regress if the IBD is surgically removed, but some studies have shown no benefit at all. There has been limited success in treating this complication with colchicine, a medication that has been available for many, many years to treat acute gout. For patients in whom the progression of amyloidosis cannot be halted, dialysis and kidney transplantation remain possible alternatives.

Eye Problems

Eye disease, associated with either IBD or its treatment, occurs in about 10 percent of patients, though many cases are mild and are not brought to a doctor's attention. There are three main inflammatory conditions: conjunctivitis, episcleritis, and iritis (also known as uveitis). Cataracts can occur as a complication of steroid therapy (see Chapter 6).

The occurrence of these inflammatory conditions may not correspond to how active the bowel disease is. Inflammation in the eye usually requires local treatment, which is often in the form of steroid drops.

Conjunctivitis (inflammation of the membrane lining and bordering the eyelids) is the most common condition, but it is not absolutely clear that this is a feature of IBD, since it is also common in the general population. Conjunctivitis can be unpleasant, but it is not serious.

Episcleritis (inflammation of the white of the eye) occurs in 3 to 4 percent of IBD patients, mostly those with Crohn's colitis. Patients usually complain of burning in one eye, and increased tear production. There may be some mild localized redness. This condition is also minor.

Iritis (inflammation of the colored part of the eye), which occurs in 0.5 to 3 percent of patients, mainly in males with ulcerative colitis, can lead to serious loss of vision and requires treatment by an ophthalmologist. People with iritis suddenly develop blurred vision, headaches, and eye pain. In rare cases, this problem can occur repeatedly. There is considerable controversy about how to treat this condition.

Blood-Clotting Abnormalities

It is well recognized that some IBD patients have abnormalities of the blood-clotting mechanism, resulting in an increased tendency to form blood clots in otherwise healthy blood vessels. There are approximately thirteen different chemicals known as "clotting factors," some of which are increased in some patients with IBD. In addition, many patients have an elevated platelet count, especially during flare-ups of the bowel disease. Platelets are blood cells that are very important in the formation of blood clots.

Certain conditions predispose many sick people, with a variety of acute and chronic diseases, to develop unwanted blood clots. Patients who are bedridden or dehydrated (whether it be due to fever, vomiting, diarrhea, or any other cause) are said to be in a "hypercoagulable" state, meaning that they are more prone to unwanted clots.

Most of the clots in IBD patients are in veins. The common locations are the leg veins and pelvic veins, but veins anywhere in the body can be involved.

To some extent, this problem can be circumvented if you avoid prolonged periods of immobility. People who must stay in bed should be encouraged to wiggle their toes, bend their knees, and generally exercise their limbs. Isometric exercises are often very helpful. I always tell my patients that, when visitors come, it should not be just to talk. Visitors should be enlisted to help the patient exercise. Simple things like having the patient push each foot downward against the resistance of another person's hand can be very useful. You can easily make up similar exercises involving the use of other leg muscles or arm muscles. People not confined to bed should be encouraged to get out of bed, even if they don't feel like it.

In some situations doctors give bedridden patients low doses of anticoagulants ("blood thinners") to reduce the risk of unwanted blood clotting. The technology for doing this is quite advanced and poses little risk to the patient. If a patient does develop a clot, the usual treatment is an anticoagulant.

Pancreatitis

Inflammatory disease of the pancreas has occasionally been reported in association with IBD for many years. Many of the cases are clearly due to taking certain medications: sulfasalazine, 5-aminosalicylate, azathioprine, and 6-mercaptopurine (see Chapter 6). Other cases link pancreatitis with Crohn's disease but not ulcerative colitis.

Cancer Complicating IBD

People with either ulcerative colitis or Crohn's colitis have more risk of cancer of the colon than the general population, and people with small-bowel Crohn's disease have an increased risk of cancer of the small bowel. Detailed information on this topic is found in Chapter 10.

Nutritional Complications of IBD

Malnutrition – characterized by low body weight, sometimes with vitamin or mineral deficiencies – is a common problem. See Chapter 5 for details. See Chapter 7 for "short-bowel syndrome."

TEN

Cancer and IBD

Up till the end of the 1950s, people with ulcerative colitis, but not those with Crohn's disease, were thought to have an increased risk of colon cancer. Crohn's disease was felt to involve only the small intestine, and all colitis was felt to be ulcerative colitis. At the end of the 1950s and the beginning of the 1960s, however, medical researchers concluded that Crohn's disease could occur in the colon, though it was uncommon. Now we know that Crohn's disease not only occurs in the colon, but is common there.

It is now generally accepted that the cancer risk in Crohn's colitis is probably the same as the cancer risk for ulcerative colitis. People with small-bowel Crohn's disease also have an increased risk of small-bowel cancer. However, cancer of the small intestine is extremely rare in the general population. Even with the increased risk associated with Crohn's disease, it is still a very uncommon event.

Who Is at Risk?

Ulcerative Colitis

Two factors determine the risk of cancer in people with ulcerative colitis: how much of the colon is (or has been) inflamed, and the total duration of the disease.

Generally speaking, the more colon involved, the greater the risk. People who have proctitis (colitis limited to the rectum) have a risk equal to that of the general population. Over the past several years we've learned that colon cancer is at least partly genetically determined. There are therefore two groups in the "general population": those with no family history of colon polyps (the forerunners of most colon cancers) or colon cancer; and those with a family history of colon polyps and/or cancer. It is likely that a family history of colon polyps and/or colon cancer has a significant effect on the colon-cancer risk in people with either kind of colitis.

The risk of cancer is also thought to increase with every year that passes from the time the disease began. During the first ten years of disease this risk is just fractionally above that of the general population. After ten years the risk rises, but it is still a lot less than we thought in the past. Actual numbers aren't given because there is such wide variation in the medical literature.

Crohn's Disease

The age of the person at the time Crohn's disease first began is felt to be the most important factor in determining cancer risk in people with Crohn's colitis. Those diagnosed prior to age twenty are at the greatest risk. However, the magnitude of the risk is uncertain. The extent and duration of the disease (independent of age at onset) may also be factors in colon-cancer risk, but these are not as well established as in ulcerative colitis.

As for cancer of the small bowel in people with small-bowel Crohn's disease, we still don't know the factors that influence the risk, with one exception.

Up to about 40 years ago, an operation known as "exclusion bypass" – the diseased ileum was not removed, but the normal ileum upstream was disconnected and reconnected to the colon – was performed on some patients with small-bowel Crohn's disease. This operation is no longer done, but there are still some people who have had the surgery. There have been several reports of cancer developing in the piece of excluded ileum. Because the flow of intestinal contents is diverted and does not pass through this part of the ileum, symptoms and signs of this cancer usually appear late and the area is difficult to investigate with a scope or barium enema. It is now felt that if someone who previously had an exclusion bypass is having abdominal surgery for any reason, the excluded section of ileum should be removed to eliminate any chance of cancer in this area.

Reducing the Risk

From the late 1970s, colonoscopy became more and more commonplace and easier and easier to do. It seemed obvious that examining the colon at regular intervals would lead to earlier cancer detection. Also in the late 1970s, two British pathologists named Morson and Pang described a microscopic change referred to as *dysplasia* (a change in cell architecture) in the colon biopsies of patients with colitis and early cancer. A progression from low-grade (mild) dysplasia to high-grade (severe) dysplasia to cancer was found, and was thought to have some value in predicting which patients were likely to go on to get colon cancer. Now we know that if the colon is completely removed in people with high-grade dysplasia, about half of them will turn out to have cancer; in some cases it is not visible through an endoscope, and can only be detected by a pathologist looking through a microscope.

Nevertheless, surveillance testing is extremely controversial. In this age of concern about healthcare costs, it is not at all clear that surveillance colonoscopy is "cost effective" in people with chronic colitis, be it ulcerative or Crohn's. Some studies show a relative inability to detect precancerous disease either with the endoscope or under the microscope. Other studies report that regular surveillance colonoscopy has led to the early diagnosis of cancer or even precancer.

Some medications are also believed to reduce the risk of colon cancer. These include 5-aminosalicylate (5-ASA) for both ulcerative and Crohn's colitis, and ursodeoxycholic acid, a drug sometimes given to people with sclerosing cholangitis (see Chapter 9).

How Often Should Surveillance Colonoscopy Be Done?
Just as there is no agreement about whether surveillance colonoscopy should be done at all, there is no agreement about how often it should be done. Some gastroenterologists do the procedure once a year. Others do it once every two years. Still others do a full colonoscopy every two years, with a flexible sigmoidoscopy in the years in between. Patients with total colitis often have significant shortening of their colon, and flexible sigmoidoscopy has a good chance of screening at least the lower half (left side plus part of transverse) of the colon. There is some evidence that a person who has cancer or high-grade dysplasia on the right side of the colon will also have dysplasia on the left side.

If a patient has less than half the colon affected by colitis, some gastroenterologists do surveillance examinations less frequently. There is no question that a cancer risk still exists for people with involvement of a third to half of the colon, but most experts think the risk is smaller, and the enthusiasm of both the patient and the doctor is understandably less. Nevertheless, some gastroenterologists still examine the colon every year. If the colitis is clearly confined to the rectum and sigmoid, some gastroenterologists don't do surveillance at all; others do. Only when the disease is clearly confined to the rectum is there general agreement that surveillance colonoscopy is not necessary.

What about People with Small-Bowel Crohn's Disease?
There is no equivalent surveillance procedure for small-bowel Crohn's disease. Enteroscopy (endoscopic examination of the small intestine) is impractical, and is restricted to certain patients. Some gastroenterologists X-ray the small bowel once every few years even if you are well, but the chance of picking up an asymptomatic cancer in this way is tiny.

Fortunately, small-bowel cancer, even in people with Crohn's disease, is very uncommon.

ELEVEN

Living with IBD

The theme of the present is empowerment. In medicine, knowledge is the key to empowerment. The previous chapters have provided you with general information about your problem. This one focuses on more personal issues and suggests ways for dealing with these.

Sex and IBD

As with virtually any chronic disease, someone with IBD is concerned about three main aspects of sex: sexual activity; fertility; contraception.

Sexual Activity

Understandably, a disease that has symptoms of abdominal pain, urgent and frequent bowel movements, and difficulty getting to the bathroom on time can lead to decreased interest in sexual intercourse for both men and women.

Unfortunately, both doctors and patients tend to avoid talking about sexual activity. However, if a chronic problem is interfering with a sexual relationship, the issue should be considered important enough to warrant discussion and perhaps a change in therapy.

The Impact of Surgery on Sexual Activity

As a result of improved general health after diseased bowel is removed, surgery generally brings an increased libido and improved sexual relationships. However, certain types of surgery clearly produce psychological difficulties.

Most people adapt well to a standard Brooke ileostomy and appliance (see Chapter 7), but concern over body image can result in great anxiety, which in turn can interfere significantly with sexual activity. This is especially true in young singles.

One of the most distressing things that can happen to someone with a Brooke ileostomy is that the appliance can suddenly become dislodged, or can leak during sexual intercourse. Coping with this requires maturity and a "grin and bear it" attitude. Understandably, if this happens even once, the fear that it will happen again is strongly inhibiting. Fortunately, ileostomy appliances have improved significantly over the years, and such events are uncommon.

People with a properly functioning Kock (continent) ileostomy are usually not troubled by leaking stool. However, men undergoing total colectomy to establish a continent ileostomy have approximately a 2 percent risk of impotence. This is because the nerves that control erection are in the same vicinity as those to the anus and rectum; nerve damage during surgery can be a complication.

Women undergoing total colectomy frequently develop increased vaginal fluid production without signs of infection. In many of these cases, this results in a rather heavy vaginal discharge that is annoying, at least. About one in four women who have had a total colectomy complains of painful sexual intercourse – twice as many as the number of women with this complaint before such surgery. Similarly, men may complain of reduced libido and sexual satisfaction after such surgery. However, despite these problems, the majority of total-colectomy patients report an overall improvement in their sex life.

Men undergoing a near-total colectomy with pelvic-pouch procedure and ileo-anal anastomosis have a 1 to 2 percent risk of impotence. There is also a 3 to 4 percent risk of retrograde ejaculation (see Chapter 7). Because this type of surgery is often associated with mild diarrhea and episodes of incontinence, both men and women may feel anxious during sexual intercourse. Nevertheless, as with other types of surgery, sexual life generally improves overall, likely due to better general health.

Fertility

Most studies of patients with unoperated ulcerative colitis have shown no evidence of impaired fertility in either men or women. (For possible fertility problems in women who have had a pelvic-pouch procedure, see Chapter 7.) Not so for Crohn's disease. Women with *active* Crohn's disease are somewhat less likely to become pregnant and men with *active* Crohn's disease who are in ill health or undernourished may have difficulty fathering a child.

We don't know what causes reduced fertility in women with Crohn's disease. It may be that the bowel disease somehow creates blockages of the fallopian tubes. However, fertility may actually be normal, and the reduced number of pregnancies may be a result of either medical advice to avoid pregnancy or such severe pain on intercourse that it is avoided.

There is some evidence that people with Crohn's disease who are treated surgically may have higher fertility than those who are treated with drugs and/or diet therapy. Presumably this relates to improved general health. If general health improved sufficiently without surgery, the same improvement might be seen.

Sulfasalazine (see Chapter 6) can reduce the sperm count enough to result in male infertility. Fortunately this abnormality is reversible, though it takes two to three months for the sperm count to return to normal after the drug is stopped. None of the other medications commonly used for IBD is known to interfere with fertility.

Contraception

All forms of contraception can be used by patients with IBD.

There is no evidence that the birth control pill interacts with any of the medications used to treat IBD, but there is evidence that it may aggravate the symptoms of some women with IBD. However, this is controversial and is certainly not a reason to avoid the pill. If you are on the pill and you are wondering if you should stop it, discuss this with your gastroenterologist.

The Menstrual Cycle and IBD

Recent studies have shown that women with irritable bowel syndrome (see Chapter 4) are likely to experience an increase in their symptoms just before and during menstrual periods. Similarly, many women with IBD complain that their symptoms become worse when they get their period. But this has not been well studied to date, and strategies to help them deal with the problem have not yet been designed.

Pregnancy and IBD

Here are some commonly asked questions, and some answers.

What Effect Can My IBD Have on a Pregnancy?

Ulcerative colitis and Crohn's disease generally do not have any major adverse effects on pregnancy. Most babies are normal and full-term, but about one-quarter of babies born to Crohn's mothers will have a low birth weight. Deliveries are no more complicated than usual and there is no increase in the need for forceps or caesarian section.

If the disease is active *before* conception, the risks of a miscarriage or premature birth are slightly increased, more so in Crohn's disease than in ulcerative colitis. If a severe attack of IBD occurs *during* a pregnancy, the chances for a normal delivery and a healthy baby are slightly reduced. If the symptoms of ulcerative colitis *first* occur during a pregnancy, the chances for a normal delivery and a healthy baby are very good.

Crohn's disease that appears for the first time during pregnancy may have a poorer outcome. However, in comparison with ulcerative colitis, there have been relatively few reports of Crohn's disease beginning during pregnancy. When it has been reported, there has been a significantly higher rate of fetal death. This information applies *only* to Crohn's disease that appears for the *first* time during pregnancy.

Does Pregnancy Increase the Risk of a Flare-up of IBD?
For anyone in remission, there is a 30 percent chance of a relapse during the next year. Pregnancy neither increases nor reduces that chance. If a flare-up does occur around this time, it will more likely happen in the first three months of pregnancy or soon after delivery. The behavior of the disease during one pregnancy cannot be used to predict what will happen in another pregnancy in the same woman.

Women with Crohn's disease who have had surgery for Crohn's reportedly do much better during pregnancy than those who have never had surgery.

If My IBD Is Active When I Become Pregnant, What Effect Will the Pregnancy Have on the Disease?
If your disease is active at the time of conception, generally it

will continue to be active during pregnancy. As when you are not pregnant, therapy should be aimed at controlling the disease.

Can Pregnancy Affect the Course of My IBD?
A recent study has suggested that women with Crohn's and a previous pregnancy need surgery to remove diseased areas less often than those who have never been pregnant.

What about Abortion and IBD?
There is no evidence that therapeutic abortions carry any greater risks for women who have IBD than for those who don't. If pregnancy occurs while a woman is on the antibiotic metronidazole or on methotrexate, a therapeutic abortion may be recommended. In rare instances, a pregnancy may be terminated in a woman with severe active IBD.

Do Women with IBD Need a Special Diet during Pregnancy?
Generally speaking, the normal, well-balanced diet that any pregnant woman should follow is fine. If your disease is active, however, you may have to pay extra attention to your diet. The most important thing is to make sure you are taking in enough energy for the fetus to develop and grow normally. Failure to gain weight at the expected rate is a sign that more energy is needed. Inflammation uses up energy, so extra intake may be necessary. Pregnant patients can be adequately nourished with enteral diets or total parenteral nutrition (see Chapter 5) if necessary.

Can I Take My IBD Drugs When I'm Pregnant?
Like anyone else, IBD patients should try to avoid *unnecessary* drugs during pregnancy. Fortunately, sulfasalazine has proved safe for the fetus. There is no increased risk of prematurity, stillbirth, fetal deformity, or other congenital abnormalities. There

is no increased danger of a full-term infant becoming jaundiced if you take sulfasalazine to the end of your pregnancy. But be sure to notify your baby's doctor if you are on sulfasalazine, steroids, or narcotic medications.

It's very likely that 5-ASA will prove safe in pregnancy, but we don't know yet. Because 5-ASA is a component of sulfasalazine, and sulfasalazine, as we've said, is safe in pregnancy, there is every reason to believe that 5-ASA is also safe. Reports so far have attested to the safety of this agent.

For the past twenty years or so, steroids have been considered safe in pregnancy, but recent studies have suggested that there is a very small risk of fetal deformity over and above the usual risk in the non-IBD population. This doesn't mean you should avoid steroids in pregnancy, only that there should (as always) be a good reason for taking them.

In the past, immunosuppressive medications such as azathioprine and 6-mercaptopurine were generally not recommended during pregnancy, but several centers have reported statistics suggesting that the risk to the fetus, if any, is small. The current thinking is that if you are on azathioprine or 6-mercaptopurine when you become pregnant, and your IBD is under control, you should *not* stop these medications, since disease activity is a greater potential risk to your baby than the drug. As noted earlier, therapeutic abortion may be recommended where the mother has been taking either methotrexate or metronidazole; indeed, methotrexate has been used (in large doses) to produce a therapeutic abortion.

The situation with ciprofloxacin is unclear; it is potentially capable of causing limb and joint abnormalities in the fetus, but there are reports of healthy babies born to mothers who stayed on the drug.

We don't have information about the safety of diphenoxylate and loperamide in pregnancy because no studies have been done.

Codeine, the main alternative to these drugs, *has* been studied, and is associated with a very slight increase in risk to the fetus.

Can I Breastfeed My Baby?

If your disease is active at the time of delivery, you may not be able to provide sufficient milk. Sulfasalazine and 5-ASA do make their way into breast milk, but they present no hazard to the full-term infant if you are able to breastfeed. In rare cases the breastfed infant has had diarrhea because the mother was taking 5-ASA (tablets, enemas, or suppositories).

Steroids and antidiarrheal drugs also make their way into breast milk, and may cause side effects in infants. The risk is directly related to the dose. If you want to nurse your baby while you are on any of these drugs, the baby should be carefully monitored by the baby's doctor. No information is available on the safety of loperamide during breastfeeding.

It was thought in the past that you should not breastfeed on immunosuppressive drugs or the antibiotic metronidazole, but there is some evidence that the danger has been overestimated. Nevertheless, these drugs *do* get into your baby's bloodstream. It may be recommended to reduce your immunosuppressive dosage, and possibly to monitor your child's white blood count. These issues should be discussed with your doctor.

Life Expectancy

Over the past 30 years, the life expectancy of people with IBD has approached that of the general population. This is attributable to several factors, including earlier diagnosis, a greater range of therapies, better attention to nutrition, better surgical techniques, and much better care following surgery.

From a statistical point of view, the first attack of colitis (either type) is often the worst the person will experience. The risk of dying from an attack of acute colitis has become extremely low. In fact, the only measurable risk is associated with first attacks.

Ulcerative Colitis

Of people who initially have ulcerative proctitis, between 10 and 20 percent can expect to progress to more involvement of the colon, usually within the first two years but occasionally even after that. Of those who have ulcerative colitis involving the rectum and sigmoid colon, up to 50 percent may progress to more involvement of the colon, usually during the first ten years of disease. The percentage of people dying from ulcerative colitis has steadily declined over the past 30 years; the risk is greater than that of the general population only with the first attack. The lifetime risk of requiring colectomy is about 30 percent. However, people with extensive colitis will need surgery more than those with limited disease.

Crohn's Disease

Studies over the years have consistently shown a higher mortality risk in Crohn's disease than in ulcerative colitis. However, just as the risk of dying from ulcerative colitis has decreased greatly in the past 30 years, the same is true for Crohn's disease. It is currently thought that the mortality risk is close to that of the general population. There appears to be a modest increase in this risk during the first five years of the disease, in people who require multiple operations, and in those whose disease begins at a young age. Part of the increased risk of dying in this latter group appears to be related to the development of cancer.

In the long term, patients with Crohn's disease can expect surgery much more often than those with ulcerative colitis. Among people with all forms of Crohn's disease, the probability of requiring some kind of surgery is about 80 percent. The average number of operations per patient in this group is

approximately three. But these statistics include minor operations, such as draining a peri-anal abscess. Patients with small-
bowel Crohn's disease who have had more than a yard (about
a meter) of ileum removed are much more likely to have gallbladder stones and/or kidney stones than the general population, or than patients with Crohn's disease who have not had
this extent of surgery.

Quality of Life with IBD

"Quality of life" has become an important measuring-stick for
evaluating the effects of chronic diseases, and of various treatments. In the 1980s a group at McMaster University in Hamil-
ton, Ontario, developed a quality-of-life index to evaluate
patients with inflammatory bowel disease. This index has been
used in a variety of studies, both nationally and internationally.

The index has proved to be extremely useful in assessing
quality of life for people with IBD. The index is not all-
inclusive – items related to sexual activity and satisfaction are
noteworthy by their absence. Nevertheless, studies have shown
that the index score before and after medical or surgical treatment provides a relatively accurate assessment of the benefit,
or lack of benefit, to the patient.

Statistics can be very helpful, but in the end it comes down
to each individual. A drug or surgical procedure that benefits most patients may not be looked on favorably by a given
person. Furthermore, in studying any treatment choice,
measuring the quality-of-life index *over a period of time* is
desirable.

Let's take someone who has been continuously ill with
Crohn's disease for several months. She is chronically fatigued,
eating poorly, and taking multiple medications. Surgery is
advised and performed. One month following surgery, she is
feeling much better, is off almost all medications, and is eating

Quality-of-Life Index

This index evaluates quality of life according to five factors:

1. *Bowel symptoms*
   a) frequent bowel movements
   b) loose bowel movements
   c) abdominal cramps
   d) pain in the abdomen
   e) abdominal bloating
   f) passing large amounts of gas

2. *Systemic symptoms*
   a) fatigue
   b) overall feeling unwell
   c) feeling worn out
   d) tiring very easily
   e) waking up during the night
   f) feeling weak

3. *Emotional function*
   a) frustrated
   b) depressed
   c) discouraged
   d) fearful of not finding a washroom in time
   e) worried about surgery
   f) worried about flare-up
   g) irritable
   h) angry
   i) anxious
   j) impatient

4. *Social impairment*
   a) avoiding events where washrooms are not close at hand
   b) canceling social engagements
   c) being unable to play sports
   d) being unable to plan outings in advance

5. *Functional impairment*
   a) being unable to attend work/school regularly
   b) having to stop work/school
   c) having difficulty doing housework

well, and her quality of life is clearly much improved. She does have diarrhea, which is a result of the surgery, but she has been told that this is usually temporary and so she is optimistic.

Six months later the diarrhea has not gotten any better and she is now being told that this diarrhea – a result of surgery, not of Crohn's disease – is likely to be permanent, and that medication will be necessary to keep it under control. A quality-of-life measurement taken at this point is not as good. Three months later, she develops symptoms indicating that the Crohn's disease has recurred. Over the next few weeks she does poorly, develops an abscess, and is told that another operation will be necessary. At this point her quality of life is greatly colored by what has happened and what is going to happen, and the score is significantly reduced.

After the second operation, the patient is pessimistic. But as it turns out, there is no evidence of recurring Crohn's disease for the next five years. As the woman acclimatizes to chronic diarrhea requiring antidiarrheal therapy, her quality-of-life score steadily improves.

Other Factors Affecting Quality of Life

Losses

Developing a chronic disease may mean certain losses for the sufferer. If the disease is mild, losses will be minimal. However, if you are frequently or continuously ill the effects on life in general are likely to be significant. Unfortunately, personal relationships frequently suffer. It is not unusual for a healthy spouse to be unable to cope with chronic illness in a partner. Unmarried patients generally find it more difficult to establish lasting relationships. They may be embarrassed about the disease, or unable to participate in various activities because of restrictions the disease places on them, or may lack sufficient energy to engage in certain activities with a potential partner. Having a chronic illness sometimes means a loss of independence. People who are frequently ill, especially if the illness requires hospitalization, need to depend on someone else to deal with such simple things as paying bills. One of the hardest things for most patients to accept is at least intermittent loss of the ability to control their own lives.

Anger
When older people develop a chronic illness, they may be upset, but they tend to accept it more easily than young people. As people get older, they see family and friends developing illnesses and expect to have some sort of problem sooner or later. Conversely, young people generally assume that everyone else in their age group is healthy, and their feeling is "Why me?" Of course, it's not true that all young people are well. Many young people have friends who have severe asthma and end up in emergency departments on a regular basis. Others have friends with severe diabetes who must inject insulin every day. Still others have friends who have leukemia or some other form of cancer. Nevertheless it is true that most young people are healthy, and certainly the image of youth is constantly linked with the idea of health and energy in our culture.

Particularly in the initial stages of disease, the patient is likely to feel anger toward family, friends, and healthcare workers, all of whom are trying to be helpful but cannot know exactly how that person feels. Even when they are coping well, some patients are angry and frequently feel that "people don't understand." This may apply, in the patient's mind, to parents, teachers, co-workers, relatives, and friends. To some extent, this perception of a lack of understanding is true. Even if teachers or co-workers are told the name of the disease (and patients don't always want to advertise their problems), many people have no good understanding of what effects such diseases have on a person's life.

Especially when IBD is resistant to treatment, patients feel that days are like weeks and weeks are like months or years. They often temporarily lose confidence in their ability to overcome an attack of the illness. This pessimistic attitude and frustration with the disease may lead them to ignore treatment instructions, or at least to be careless about them.

Coping Strategies

If you have a chronic illness such as Crohn's disease or ulcerative colitis, there are many ways you can improve your situation and develop a more positive outlook.

First, accept the fact that you have the disease. Then try to learn about it. Learn about the treatments. Think of yourself and your healthcare providers as a team. Help them to help you; in this way you will help yourself. As has been said many times in relation to many other problems, take one day at a time.

When you feel well, eat well. Consider that a little extra weight is like money in the bank. Unless you are clearly overweight, don't worry about gaining a few extra pounds. When your disease flares up and you lose weight, you will not be as badly off.

When you are in the hospital, try not to think of it as a prison. Get permission to go outside, weather permitting. Having an IV line, including a central line, does not mean you have to stay indoors. Even patients with various drainage tubes, drainage bags, bladder catheters, and other devices can go out. If you are on a tube feeding, don't be embarrassed and hide in your room. Getting out into fresh air (even polluted air!) improves outlook. Whether you are roaming the halls of the hospital or strolling outside, remind yourself that exercise is good for you. The more you strengthen your muscles, the more rapidly you will recover from the illness or operation that has led to your hospitalization.

If you are weak, the philosophy should be that *any* activity is better than no activity. I tell patients who are very weak to start by just sitting on the edge of the bed. The next step is to stand beside the bed, and after that to get out on one side of the bed, walk around the bed, and get in on the other side. I have had patients start out with limited activity such as this and end up literally running up and down the stairs of the hospital – carrying an IV pole! Being active has psychological rewards as well as physical ones. And there are other things you can do for yourself in hospital to make it feel more like home. Have family or friends bring your schoolwork, office work, or other work. If you have a portable computer (insured!), have them bring it in. Wear your own clothes, use your own pillow, and have someone bring you soft toilet paper!

If you know that antidiarrheal drugs effectively control your diarrhea or the urgency to go the bathroom, use them to give you psychological security when you are going out, whether to the theater, a sports event, a party, or simply the grocery store. Similarly, such medications can be helpful in sexual activity.

Be self-reliant. Learn which kinds of medical decisions you can make on your own. Don't feel that you have to ask your doctor everything. This will build your self-confidence and help to make you feel better.

Financial Effects of Chronic Disease
Perhaps one of the most difficult areas in maintaining quality of life is the financial burden of chronic disease. Health plans

may take care of hospital costs and a few outpatient expenses, but some people don't have a health plan, and other people have plans that cover only part of the cost of medications, many of which are quite expensive. Disability insurance that adequately replaces a person's income is extremely expensive and inaccessible to many people. Some pharmaceutical companies recognize these financial difficulties and provide free medication to the patient via the physician. However, during difficult economic times, when many individuals cannot afford the cost of medications, the demand greatly exceeds the supply. Not only does illness interfere with income, it also frequently makes it impossible to put any money away for retirement. This can obviously have far-reaching consequences for patients and their families.

Social Effects

A Danish study reviewed familial, social, and professional data on a group of patients with ulcerative colitis in comparison with a control group of patients of similar age and sex who were in hospital for a variety of acute illnesses. A higher percentage of colitis patients had university degrees, and fewer were unskilled workers. Patients had generally kept the same job for equal lengths of time in both groups. The colitis patients had the same frequency of marriage as the controls and seemed to have no more familial or sexual problems. The authors of this study constructed a score to rate social life. They included such items as frequency of visiting friends, and participating in cultural events, sports events, etc. About a third of the patients in both groups had very active social lives and about half had moderately active social lives; no differences were found between the ulcerative colitis patients and the controls. Similarly, a score was devised for physical activity, and again no difference was found. The authors concluded that patients with ulcerative colitis, despite their often troublesome disease, can lead normal lives, provided that they have access to appropriate medical and surgical care when they are ill.

Statistics related to family and social life are not as readily available for Crohn's disease. However, the overall quality of life is not as good, *on average*, for Crohn's patients as for ulcerative colitis patients. But of course both diseases appear in a wide spectrum, from something that is a minor nuisance to something that is a cause of major ongoing disability.

Parents and Children, Children and Parents

Most parents can adjust to chronic disease in themselves, and most children can do the same. However, when parents have to adjust to chronic illness in their children, there is sometimes an extreme tendency to be overprotective. At the same time the sick child goes into denial of illness, and becomes quite resistant to parental intervention.

Parents must try to allow the patient to develop a relationship with the doctor, particularly when the patient is a teenager or a young adult. Parents must give their children a chance to manage their disease independently, in the same way that they must learn to "let go" as healthy children grow up. By the same token, children should recognize that their parents genuinely care and are trying to help.

Parents – trust your kids! Be there to help them when they want help. Kids – respect your parents! If you want independence, show that you can be responsible. Take your medications without having to be reminded. Tell your doctor (and your parents) when you are sick. Keep your appointments.

Quality of life is, to a large extent, a personal perception. It reflects the way a particular individual feels about his or her state of health as well as various other aspects of life in general. Many people expect to feel good all the time. Those with IBD learn to recognize that this isn't possible. Accepting that there are going to be some "down times" is an important step in developing the ability to cope successfully with IBD. Patients who can learn self-reliance will be less tied to their doctors, and this will give them self-confidence and higher self-esteem.

Travel Tips

If you have taken the time to learn about your disease and its treatments, and to learn which medications you can start or adjust on your own and when you should use these medications, you should feel confident about traveling. Remember, many countries have IBD societies or foundations, and their members will be only too happy to help you get appropriate care should you need it. Many European countries have at least one hospital with English-speaking staff. Because IBD occurs worldwide, there are physicians and surgeons familiar with the condition worldwide.

Many knowledgeable IBD patients are aware that they can deal with most problems on their own. Sometimes all it takes is a telephone call or e-mail to your gastroenterologist back home, for a little advice or to act as a "sounding board."

Don't forget your drugs, and take adequate supplies in your carry-on luggage. If you start to experience symptoms, act promptly. People frequently wait to see if a problem will just "settle down on its own." Generally speaking, this is not a good idea when you are away from home.

If you have ulcerative colitis and you begin to have a flare-up, you can increase your oral 5-ASA, start 5-ASA suppositories or enemas, or start a steroid foam or liquid steroid enemas. If you are familiar with the use of oral steroids and think they are necessary, you can start taking them, provided your symptoms are typical and not dramatic. *If you think you are having a severe attack of colitis, seek medical advice locally.* High fever, vomiting, severe abdominal pain, and heavy bleeding are all signs of a potentially severe attack. If you treat yourself for a flare-up of colitis and then become very constipated, you can get your bowels moving again by using mineral oil or one of the other remedies described in Chapter 6.

If you have small-bowel Crohn's disease and think you are developing an obstruction, promptly put yourself on clear fluids. Keep them up for 36 to 48 hours, then gradually begin eating again, but leave roughage out of your diet for a few additional days. If you are on steroids, you should usually double the dose for a few days. You can go back to your previous dose if you settle down quickly, or taper back to your usual dose if you settle down slowly. If you are not on steroids, you will likely get over an obstruction just as fast without starting them. *If your pain is worse than usual, different from usual, or more persistent than usual, seek prompt medical assistance.*

If you have Crohn's disease and you develop symptoms of a flare-up without symptoms of obstruction, you are still likely to benefit by going on clear fluids for 36 to 48 hours. Many people with Crohn's disease feel better if they don't eat. Just resting the bowel for a few days may be sufficient treatment. If the symptoms subside but promptly begin again when you start eating, you will clearly need medication, possibly steroids. Again, many knowledgeable patients start steroids on their own in this situation. If you are on a maintenance dose of a 5-ASA product, doubling the dose may be helpful, with steroid use as a "fall-back" position. Once again, *if the flare-up is different from usual or more severe than usual, seek medical help promptly.*

If you know what's happening, it is reasonable to try to treat yourself. If you can afford to go on a trip, you should be able to afford a telephone call to your gastroenterologist for a bit of advice or reassurance. If you don't know what's happening or you are not sure, it is foolish to take chances. In this situation, seek prompt medical assistance. If you feel it would be useful for the local doctor to speak to your gastroenterologist, you can request this and offer to pay for the communication, be it a phone call or a fax.

Employers and IBD

Crohn's disease, and to a lesser extent ulcerative colitis, has always had a bad reputation in the business world. Many employers are reluctant to hire people with IBD, although this discrimination is illegal. The perception is that the IBD patient will be ill frequently and will miss work. In fact, this may never happen. Patients and their doctors have become so good at dealing with most IBD problems on an outpatient basis that many people can keep working when they are ill, with the loss of very few days, if any.

In many ways, IBD patients are ideal employees. Most become toughened by the illness and are more likely to come to work when suffering relatively minor illnesses which would keep many otherwise healthy people at home. IBD patients are conscious of the risk of a flare-up and of having to miss significant periods of work. As a result, they try not to miss work for any other reason.

Studies have been done to examine discrimination against people with Crohn's disease in both school and the workplace. In one study, students with Crohn's lost significantly more days of school than healthy students but were as successful academically, as measured by the courses they completed and whether they entered university. Although discrimination against a potential employee on the basis of an illness is illegal, many Crohn's patients feel that they have been rejected for this reason, even though another excuse may have been given. As a result of such experiences, up to 30 percent of Crohn's patients conceal their illness from employers.

Insurance and IBD

For many years patients and their physicians have known that IBD is used as a reason to refuse insurance or to charge a high premium. Groups in several countries have studied the insurance industry's attitude to people with IBD, and also looked at the issue from the patients' point of view.

The perception in the insurance industry is that those with IBD may have some difficulty, but not a great deal of difficulty, in obtaining life insurance.

Not surprisingly, people with IBD have a different opinion, based on their own experiences. In one Canadian study of people with Crohn's disease who applied for straight life insurance, only 18 percent were accepted without an extra premium; 44 percent were asked to pay extra, and 38 percent were rejected. For the same kind of insurance, the comparable figures for patients with ulcerative colitis were 31 percent, 36 percent, and 33 percent. The authors of the study believed that some patients likely do not even bother to apply for life insurance, because they are so certain they won't get it. This is probably true.

In the same study, people with Crohn's disease applying for group insurance did surprisingly well – 83 percent were accepted. In comparison, only 65 percent of patients with ulcerative colitis said they had been accepted. Among those surveyed, only a small number with Crohn's disease had applied for individual disability insurance. Of those, 41 percent were approved at standard rates and 23 percent had to pay an additional premium. In the ulcerative colitis group, a greater number of people applied and 38 percent were rejected. Most of those who applied for group disability were accepted, but the number who applied was fairly low.

The study also looked at drug plans. For individual plans, 62 percent of people with IBD were accepted at standard rates. A small number with Crohn's had to pay an extra premium. However, about 90 percent of people with IBD applying for group drug plans were successful.

Studies in other countries have yielded similar results. Gastro-enterologists are generally aware that many IBD patients must apply to several different companies before they are accepted. When their patients apply for insurance, doctors should point out that these patients are "good citizens" – they have not lost time from work, are able to participate in community activities, and have not had much disability – if that is the case.

Patients who are rejected for one type of insurance often neglect to apply for any other type. Representatives of the insurance industry have pointed out that some of the rejections have nothing to do with the diagnosis of IBD, and are related to other factors. Unquestionably, disability and premature death due to IBD have decreased significantly in the past 50 years. From the doctors' point of view, there is only a minor difference in life expectancy between most sufferers of IBD and the general population. Yet this minor difference is important to the insurance companies, who are, after all, in business.

A Strategy for Insurance Applications

Don't be discouraged from applying for insurance just because you have been rejected for one type. And don't give up because you have been rejected by one company; fellow members of your local chapter of the Crohn's and Colitis Foundation may be able to guide you to a more empathetic insurance carrier.

If you have Crohn's disease and you've had a flare-up or surgery, it's probably a good idea to wait at least six months before applying for insurance. The longer you go without active disease, the greater the likelihood of getting regular insurance with no extra premium.

Since it is somewhat difficult for people with Crohn's disease to acquire benefits, it is important to try to stay at the same job. Before you do change employment, consider carefully whether your benefits are transferable.

Looking Ahead

R esearch into causes and treatments of IBD is moving forward on many fronts. The use of genetic engineering in laboratory animals continues to generate excitement because it is possible to create individual immunological defects – known as "gene knockout" models – allowing researchers to study one particular aspect of the immune reaction at a time. This is likely to lead to newer and better therapies.

Drug researchers are continuing to search for steroids and other drugs that act locally in the intestine and then promptly become inactivated, so that side effects are reduced. As always, chance observations, like the ones regarding nicotine and heparin (see Chapter 6), will be pursued.

The role of laparoscopic surgery (using multiple little incisions instead of one big one) in IBD is evolving. The use of strictureplasty surgery to preserve bowel has expanded; the procedure has been used recently for colon strictures, which were always resected in the past. Small-bowel transplantation is still in its infancy, but there have been more and more successful cases with long-term survival. As the use of this procedure becomes more widespread, it will represent an important step forward for patients with small-bowel Crohn's disease who require multiple resections, and for those who are already severely disabled because of a surgically shortened small bowel.

Cancer researchers are using molecular genetics and related technology to look for blood, stool or tissue tests that may replace surveillance colonoscopy. Meanwhile, virtual colonoscopy, which surveys the colon with a CT scanner, is just around the corner. While it cannot provide the tissue samples needed to look for dysplasia, it may prove to be useful in combination with blood or stool tests. You still have to clean out your bowel, but virtual colonoscopy is much faster than the endoscopic variety, and it doesn't hurt!

There is every reason to be optimistic that the causes of IBD will be found someday, and we can expect that such discoveries will lead to improved treatments and, ultimately, to cures.

SOME DRUGS COMMONLY USED BY IBD PATIENTS

Many drugs are used to treat IBD and its complications; this table focuses on those that relate most specifically to IBD. Note that some are available as generic ("no-name") products.

Drug Type	Generic Names	Brand Names
Source of 5-ASA	sulfasalazine	Azulfidine*, Salazopyrin†, S.A.S.†
	5-aminosalicylate (5-ASA, mesalamine,	Asacol, Canasa*, Dipentum, Mesasal†, Pentasa, Rowasa*,
	mesalazine, olsalazine)	Salofalk†
Glucocorticosteroids	prednisone, prednisolone hydrocortisone betamethasone	Liquid Pred Syrup*, Deltasone, Winpred† Cortenema, Cortifoam Betnesol†, Celestone, Soluspan
	budesonide	Entocort†
Immunosuppressives	azathioprine	Imuran
	6-mercaptopurine (6-MP)	Purinethol
	methotrexate	Folex*, Rheumatrex
	cyclosporine, cyclosporin A	Neoral, Sandimmune
	tacrolimus (FK-506)	Prograf
	mycophenolate mofetil	CellCept*
	thalidomide	Thalomid*
Biologicals	infliximab	Remicade
	natalizumab	Antegren
	CDP-571	Humicade
	etanercept	Enbrel*
	GM-CSF (G-CSF)	Leukine*, Neupogen
Antidiarrheals	diphenoxylate	Lomotil
	loperamide	Imodium
Bowel cleanout products	polyethylene glycol-electrolyte solution	Colyte, GoLYTELY, Klean-Prep†, NuLYTELY*, Peglyte†
	sodium phosphate solution	Fleet phospho-soda, PMS-phosphates†
Antibiotics	ciprofloxacin	Cipro
	metronidazole	Flagyl
	clarithromycin	Biaxin

*U.S.A. only
†Canada only

(continued)

Drug Type	Generic Names	Brand Names
Lactose digestive enzymes	lactase	Dairyaid*, Lactaid, Dairy Ease, Lactrase, SureLac*
Other	lidocaine	Xylocaine
	cromolyn	Gastrocrom*, Nalcrom†
	botulinum toxin A	Botox
	ursodeoxycholic acid	Ursofalk†, Actigall*

*U.S.A. only
†Canada only

Glossary

Abdominoperineal resection of the rectum: an operation to remove the rectum and anus; it requires incisions in both the abdomen and the perineum.

Abscess: a localized collection of pus (dead cells and a mixture of live and dead bacteria).

Acute: of rapid onset and short duration.

Adenocarcinoma: any cancer originating in glandular tissues such as those found in the gastrointestinal tract.

Adhesions: bands of scar tissue that are usually a result of surgery, and connect the area of surgery to another structure such as a section of intestine, or the peritoneum.

Anal canal: the channel connecting the rectum to the outside world.

Anal sphincter: a ring of muscle surrounding the anal canal, controlling the opening and closing of the anus.

Anastomosis: a surgically created connection of separate or severed tubular hollow organs.

Anemia: abnormally low level of red blood cells or hemoglobin in the blood.

Anus: the lower opening of the anal canal.

Appliance: the plastic bag used to collect stool coming out of an ileostomy or colostomy.

ASA: the drug acetylsalicylic acid.

Ascending colon: section of colon running from the ileocecal valve to the hepatic flexure.

Aylett procedure: an operation used for ulcerative colitis in the 1950s, involving removal of the colon and attachment of the ileum to the rectum.

Barium enema: an X-ray examination of the colon, and sometimes the end of the ileum, using a suspension of barium sulfate, which appears white on X-ray film.

Biliary: pertaining to bile, a fluid that delivers bile salts to the small intestine to help digestion of fat, and carries some toxins and waste from the liver into the bowel; the bile ducts ("biliary tree") extend from inside the liver to the duodenum.

Biologicals: a new class of drugs that target specific molecules in the inflammatory process.

Biopsy: a tissue sample removed for examination under a microscope. An entire area of tissue may be removed, or only a little bit. Although biopsies are often taken to look for cancer, many other tissue abnormalities are also diagnosed through biopsy.

Brooke ileostomy: most commonly used form of ileostomy, invented by British surgeon Bryan Brooke. *See* **Ileostomy.**

Capsule endoscopy: a new method for examining the small intestine. A tiny camera in a capsule is swallowed, and images are later downloaded onto a computer.

CAT scan: computerized axial tomography, which takes X-rays of "slices" of the body; also known as CT scan.

CD: Crohn's disease.

Cecum: a large, blind pouch, forming the beginning of the colon on the lower right side of the abdomen, where the appendix is.

Chronic: lasting for a long time or frequently recurring.

Colectomy: surgical removal of part or all of the colon; often specified as **total** (including the rectum; also called "proctocolectomy"), or **subtotal** (excluding the rectum).

Colitis: inflammation of the colon.

Colon: the large intestine (or large bowel), extending from the cecum to the rectum, though the rectum is often referred to separately.

Colonoscopy: an examination of the colon with a flexible instrument inserted into the rectum.

Constipation: bowel movements that are harder or less frequent than normal; may also refer to passage of an inadequate volume of stool.

CT scan: *see* **CAT scan.**

Cyclosporine: an immunosuppressive drug best known for preventing rejection of transplanted organs; lower doses have been studied in patients with IBD.

Descending colon: part of the colon running down the left side, from the splenic flexure to the sigmoid colon.

Diarrhea: bowel movements that are softer, looser, or more frequent than normal.

Duodenum: the first part of the small intestine, starting at the lower end of the stomach and extending to the jejunum.

Elemental diet: a sterilized manufactured diet including protein (as amino acids) and carbohydrate (as glucose) and vitamins, minerals, and a small amount of fat. This diet requires little or no digestion.

Endoscope: an instrument used to examine the inside of a part of the body.

Enteral diet: Strictly speaking, any diet taken by mouth, as opposed to a parenteral diet, which is administered intravenously. But the term is applied to a sterilized manufactured liquid diet which may be drunk or administered through a tube into the stomach or intestine.

Enteritis: inflammation of the small intestine.

Enteroscopy: examination of the small intestine with an endoscope.

Enterostomal therapist: a nurse who specializes in the

care of ostomies and some of their complications; also known as an ET.

Enzymes: proteins or conjugated proteins, produced by living organisms, which speed chemical reactions such as the digestion or breakdown of other substances.

Esophagogastroduodenoscopy: examination of the esophagus, stomach, and duodenum with an endoscope; also known as OGD or EGD.

Esophagus: the swallowing tube, a muscular, tube-like structure that propels food from the throat into the stomach.

False urge: a strong but mistaken feeling that a bowel movement is going to occur; a symptom of rectal inflammation.

Feces: *see* **Stool.**

Fissure: a break in surface tissue, such as skin or mucosa; may be superficial, as in an anal fissure (a tear in the skin of the anal canal), or a deep, crack-like ulcer extending into the wall of the GI tract, as in Crohn's disease.

Fistula: an abnormal connection between two hollow structures (e.g., two segments of intestine, or a segment of intestine and the bladder), or between a hollow structure and the skin surface.

5-ASA: the drug 5-aminosalicylate.

Gastroenterologist: a medical specialist in the diagnosis and treatment of diseases of the stomach, intestines and associated organs (gastrointestinal tract).

Gastrointestinal tract: the mouth, esophagus, stomach, small intestine, large intestine (colon), rectum, anus, liver, biliary system, and pancreas.

GI tract: gastrointestinal tract.

Glucocorticoids: a family of steroid hormones, both synthetic and naturally occurring, that have anti-inflammatory properties.

Growth failure: an effect that any chronic disease may have on a child who has not finished growing. Growth is usually slowed, but may stop completely; reduced activity of the disease, especially in combination with improved nutrition, usually corrects the problem.

Hepatic flexure: a sharp bend in the colon just below the liver, where the ascending colon becomes the transverse colon.

IBD: inflammatory bowel disease, which includes Crohn's disease and ulcerative colitis.

Ileitis: any inflammation of the ileum, although the term is often used as a synonym for Crohn's disease of the ileum.

Ileocecal valve: short area of muscle thickening located where the ileum joins the colon, which controls the release of the fluid contents of the ileum into the colon.

Ileostomy: surgically created opening from the ileum to the abdominal surface, to allow stool to pass from the body into a plastic bag.

Ileum: last portion of the small intestine, extending from the jejunum to the cecum.

Immunosuppressives: a group of medications whose common characteristic is that they reduce activity of the immune system.

Inflammation: a localized protective reaction to injury or infection, characterized by pain, swelling, redness, heat and sometimes loss of function.

Irritable bowel syndrome (IBS): a disorder of the GI tract usually involving an abnormal bowel habit and abdominal discomfort. IBS can mimic some features of Crohn's disease but does not usually cause weight loss.

Jejunum: upper portion of the small intestine, connecting the duodenum to the ileum.

Kock ileostomy: an ileostomy that allows stool to be collected in an internal reservoir, called a Kock pouch, instead of an external bag; also known as a "continent ileostomy."

Kock pouch: a reservoir for stool, surgically constructed from the ileum; *see* **Kock ileostomy.**

Lactase: an enzyme in the mucosa (inner lining) of the small intestine that breaks down lactose into two simpler sugars, glucose and galactose.

Lactose: a sugar in dairy products, also found in some processed foods and medications.

Lactose intolerance: a partial or complete inability to digest lactose, generally resulting in abdominal pain, excess lower bowel gas, and sometimes diarrhea; also known as "lactase deficiency."

Lesion: a localized pathological change or injury to body tissue; a cancer is a lesion, and so is a scratch.

Leukocyte scan: a test using radioactively labeled white blood cells (leukocytes) to locate areas of inflammation.

Liquid-diet therapy: a treatment for Crohn's disease using a diet consisting entirely of sterilized liquids, mostly manufactured high-energy products; sometimes used as a nutritional source for people with ulcerative colitis, but it is not a treatment on its own.

Lymphoma: cancer arising in lymphoid tissue, which is present in many locations throughout the body, mainly as lymph glands, and is part of the immune system.

Mesentery: a fan-shaped piece of tissue that acts like a sling, holding the small intestine. Within this sling are lymph glands, fat, and blood vessels.

Modular-diet product: a manufactured product that supplies a single nutrient.

MRI: magnetic resonance imaging, a computerized imaging technique; also known as MR.

Mucosa: the inner lining of any hollow structure in the body.

Mucous fistula: a surgically created connection between part of the GI tract and the skin; it differs from an ostomy in that the portion of intestine leading to the mucous fistula is disconnected from the flow of bowel contents.

Mucus: nature's lubricant, normally produced by glands of the mucosa.

Osmosis: diffusion of a fluid across a membrane.

Ostomy: surgically created connection between two portions of the GI tract, or between a portion carrying bowel contents and the skin.

Parenteral: entering the body by a route other than the GI tract, such as by intravenous or intramuscular injection.

Parenteral nutrition: a technique of supplying nutrition directly into the bloodstream, bypassing the intestine.

Pelvic pouch: a reservoir surgically constructed from the ileum, as a substitute for the rectum.

Perforation: a hole right through the wall of a hollow structure.

Peri-anal: around the anus, but the term is also used to refer to the area within the anal canal.

Perineum: the area between the anus and the posterior boundary of the genitals.

Peritoneum: a thin, tough membrane lining the abdominal cavity and folding inward to enclose some of the abdominal organs.

Peritonitis: inflammation of the peritoneum.

Phlegmon: an infected, inflamed mass of tissue.

PN: *see* **Parenteral nutrition**.

Polymeric diet: a synthetic diet that contains food components in forms requiring at least some digestion (*see* **Elemental diet**).

Pouchitis: inflammation of either a Kock pouch or a pelvic pouch.

Proctocolectomy: *see* **Colectomy**.

Proctoscopy: examination of the rectum with an endoscope.

Rectum: the last part of the colon, from the sigmoid colon to the anal canal.

Resection: surgical removal of an organ or part of an organ.

Serosa: the outer lining of the GI tract, present everywhere except in the esophagus and the lower half of the rectum.

Short-bowel syndrome: a condition of chronic diarrhea and reduced absorption of food, due to surgical removal or bypass of a major portion of the small intestine.

Sigmoid colon: part of the colon connecting the descending colon to the rectum.

Sigmoidoscopy: examination of the rectum and sigmoid colon with an endoscope; may include some or all of the descending colon, and some of the transverse colon.

Sign: a finding made during the course of a physical examination, such as an enlarged liver.

Small-bowel enema: an X-ray examination of the small intestine in which a radiologist injects a suspension of barium sulfate through a small plastic tube which has been inserted into the intestine through the nose.

Small-bowel series: an X-ray examination of the small intestine in which the patient drinks a suspension of barium sulfate.

Sphincter: a ring of muscle that opens and closes, to control the passage of something.

Splenic flexure: part of the colon just below the spleen, where the transverse colon turns abruptly to become the descending colon.

Steroids: commonly used to refer to a large number of hormones with a similar chemical structure. They include glucocorticoid steroids (which reduce inflammation), male sex hormones (such as the so-called anabolic steroids sometimes misused by athletes), female sex hormones, and others.

Stoma: the surgically constructed opening of an ostomy.

Stool: a collective term for the various components discharged at the end of the GI tract. Whether this material comes out of the rectum, a colostomy, or an ileostomy, it is still called stool.

Stricture: an abnormal area of narrowing of a hollow organ or structure.

Strictureplasty: a surgical technique that widens an area of narrowing, instead of removing it; also known as "stricturoplasty."

Suppository: rapidly dissolving form of solid medication that is inserted through the anus into the rectum.

Symptom: something abnormal perceived by the patient, such as fatigue or pain.

Tenesmus: an intense urge to have a bowel movement, relieved partially or not at all by the passage of material from the rectum, whether it is stool, blood, or gas; frequently associated with an inability to pass anything. Tenesmus is a symptom of rectal inflammation.

Topical: medication applied directly to the area affected; a suppository is an example.

Toxic megacolon: the most serious complication of an attack of acute colitis. Some or all of the colon becomes paralyzed, and swells up with gas, stretching the wall.

TPN: total parenteral nutrition; *see* **Parenteral.**

Trace elements: elements required by the body in very tiny amounts, such as zinc and chromium.

Transverse colon: part of the colon running across the upper abdomen, from the hepatic flexure to the splenic flexure.

UC: ulcerative colitis.

Ulcer: a break in a lining; an open sore on an arm is a skin ulcer, for example. The ulcers of the small bowel or colon that occur in ulcerative colitis or Crohn's disease have nothing to do with duodenal or stomach ulcers.

Ulcerative proctitis: ulcerative colitis that only involves the rectum.

Ultrasound: a technique for examining tissues using sound waves.

Upper GI series: X-ray examination of the esophagus, stomach, and duodenum; the patient drinks a suspension of barium sulfate, and several X-rays are taken.

Further Resources

Organizations

There are chapters of the Crohn's and Colitis Foundation and the United Ostomy Association across the United States and Canada; check your telephone book for your local chapter.

United States

Crohn's and Colitis
Foundation of America
386 Park Avenue S.
17th floor
New York, NY 10016
(212)685-3440
www.ccfa.org

United Ostomy Association
of America
36 Executive Park
Suite 120
Irvine, CA 92614
(714)660-8624
www.uoa.org

Canada

Crohn's and Colitis
Foundation of Canada
21 St. Clair Avenue E.
Suite 301
Toronto, ON M4T 1L9
(416) 920-5035
Toll-free 1-800-387-1479
www.ccfc.ca

United Ostomy Association
of Canada Inc.
P.O. Box 46057
444 Yonge Street
Toronto, ON M5B 2L8
(416) 595-5452
Toll-free 1-800-826-0826
www.ostomycanada.ca

Books

Cartwright, Peter. *Probiotics for Crohn's and Colitis*. Ilford, Essex, U.K.: Prentice, 2003.

Greenwood, Jan K. *The IBD Nutrition Book*. New York: John Wiley & Sons, 1992.

Janowitz, Henry D. *Good Food for Bad Stomachs*. New York: Oxford University Press, 1998.

McFarlane, Donna. *Division of Surgery*. Toronto: Women's Press, 1994.

Meyer, Kathleen. *How to Shit in the Woods*. Berkeley, California: Ten Speed Press, 1994.

Scala, Dr. James. *The New Eating Right for a Bad Gut*. New York: Plume, 2000.

Zukerman, Eugenia, and Julie Ingelfinger. *Coping with Prednisone and Other Cortisone-Related Medicines*. New York: St. Martin's Press, 1998.

Index

Page numbers in italic indicate a figure, table, or boxed text. For brand names of medications, please see table p. 195–96.

abdomen, fullness in, *see also* bloating 21, 27
abdominal pain
  after ileostomy 109, 112
  in CD 21–22, 25–27, 143
  in toxic megacolon 148
  in UC 21
  on liquid diets 52
  with lactose intolerance 37, 39
  with strictures 148
abdominal swelling 26–27
abdominoperineal resection 105
abortion 176–77
abscesses (boils)
  after surgery 119
  chronic *140*, 141
  diagrams *136*
  how they form 135–37
  in CD 27, 150
  size 149
  treatment 137, 139, 141, 149
acetaminophen 96
acetylsalicylic acid (ASA) 96
acid-reducing drugs 98–99
ACTH 69
adhesions 141
African descent 38
age
  and cancer risk 167
  and diet 47, 56

and ileostomy 108
and illness acceptance 183
and lactose intolerance 37
and surgical treatment 113–14
when IBD begins 9
air-contrast barium enema 29–30
alcohol *81*, 82
alicaforsen 79
alpha4 integrin 78
alternative therapies *102*
5-aminosalicylate (5-ASA)
  during breastfeeding 178
  during pregnancy 177
  for cuffitis 119
  for IBD 61–62
  for reducing cancer risk 169
  side effects 62–64, 165
ampicillin 80
amyloidosis 162–63
anal canal
  anatomy and function 4
  disease in 149–51
anal fissures 91, 93–94, 150
analgesics 96
anal sphincter
  anatomy and function 4–5
  spasms 93–94
anal ulcers 91, 93–94, 150
anastomosis
  1950s (Aylett procedure) 109–10

and recurring CD 132
defined 106
for CD of the ileum 123, 125
for Crohn's colitis *130*
ileo-anal 113–20
inflammation 119
narrowing 119
anemia 99, 101, 151–53
anger 183–84
ankylosing spondylitis 12, 154–55
anti-alpha4 integrin antibodies 78
antibiotic-associated colitis *22*, 98
antibiotics
during breastfeeding 178
for abscesses 141
for CD 80–83
for fistulas 149
for mouth sores *157*
for other conditions 98
for pouchitis 118
for UC 79–80
side effects *22*, 81–84, 98
antibodies
antineutrophil cytoplasmic 12
anti-Saccharomyces cerevisiae 12
defined 13
anticoagulants 165
antidiarrheals
after surgery 117, 129
during breastfeeding 178
for IBD 88
for psychological security 185
side effects 88–89
antigens 13
anti-inflammatories 22, 96–97
anti-intercellular adhesion molecule 79
antineutrophil cytoplasmic antibodies 12
anti-Saccharomyces cerevisiae antibodies 12

antisense oligonucleotide 79
anti-tuberculosis drugs 87
anus
anatomy 4
inflamed 93–94
itchy 95–96
aphthous ulcers 156–57
appendectomy 17
appendicitis *23*, 26
appendix
anatomy and function 3, *23*
in CD 26
appetite loss
in CD 25
in toxic megacolon 148
in UC 21
resulting from dietary restrictions 55
arthralgia 154
arthritis 59, 96–98, 154
5-ASA *see* 5-aminosalicylate
ASA (acetylsalicylic acid) 96
ascending colon 3
Asian descent
and IBD 9–10
and lactose intolerance 38
Aylett procedure 109–10
azathioprine
during pregnancy 177
for IBD 72, 153
in children 144
side effects 72, 165

baby ointments 95
backwash ileitis 7–8
barium enema
air contrast 29–30
single contrast 31
bathroom trips *see* bowel movements
Beano 43
Behçet's disease *22*

bile duct cancer 160
bile-salt binders 90–91, 127
bile salts
    absorbed by ileum 3
    causing diarrhea after surgery
        125
biological drugs 74–79
biopsy 28
black people 10
bloating, *see also* gas
    after meals 25
    from lactose intolerance 37
    with strictures 148
blood
    clotting abnormalities 164–65
    in stool 19, 25, 112, 143,
        152–53
blood vessel abnormalities 16
boils *see* abscesses
bone disease 41, 155–56
bone-meal tablets 42
botulinum toxin injection 94
bowel movements
    after pelvic pouch surgery 117
    after surgery for Crohn's colitis
        129, 131–32
    and lactose intolerance 39
    false urge 19–20, 25
    normal functioning 4–5
    regulating 91–94
bran 44, 90
bread *40*
breastfeeding 178
Brooke ileostomy 107–9, *130*
budesonide 69, 118
bulk formers 89–90
bypass, exclusion 168

caffeine *22*
calcium
    importance 41, 156

maintaining intake while avoiding
        lactose 39–40
    supplements 40–42, 101, 156
calories *see* energy (calories)
cancer
    genetic factors 167, 194
    reducing the risk 168–70
    with CD 160, 165, 167–68
    with UC 120, 160, 165, 167
canker sores 156, *157*
capsule endoscopy 32
CAT (computerized axial
    tomography) scan 33–34
Caucasians 10
causes *see* risk factors
cavities 157
CD *see* Crohn's disease
CDP-571 77
cecum
    anatomy 3
    UC in 7
cefazolin 80
celecoxib 97
cellular adhesion molecules 78
cheese 40
chemotherapy *22*
chest pain 26
children
    and second-hand smoke 16
    diagnosis of IBD 34, 142–43
    diet 145
    drug therapy for IBD 143–44
    growth failure in IBD 143
    living with IBD 187–88
    nutrition 144
    psychological effects of IBD 145
    surgery for IBD 134, 144
    tube feeding 51, 144
chills 21
cholangitis 158–60
cholestyramine 91, 127

chromium supplements 101
chronic continuous colitis 21
cimetidine 99
ciprofloxacin
    during pregnancy 177
    for IBD 80–82
    side effects 82–83
cirrhosis 45
clarithromycin 83
cleansing
    of anal area 95–96
    of colon 29
codeine
    as antidiarrheal 88–89, 91
    during pregnancy 178
colectomy
    1930s and 1940s 106–7
    1950s (Aylett procedure) 109–10
    and recurring CD 133
    defined 105
    lowers cancer risk 120
    near-total 105–6
    subtotal 105, *130*
    total 105
colitis, *see also* ulcerative colitis
    antibiotic-associated *22*, 98
    chronic continuous 21
    collagenous 22
    Crohn's 24–25, 129–33
    granulomatous 6
    idiopathic 6
    indeterminate 6, 120–21
    infectious 14–15
    microscopic 22
    nonspecific 6
    severe 53
    toxic 147
collagenous colitis 22
colon
    anatomy and function 3–5
    cancer 120, 165–67

CD in 8, 24–25, 129, 133
    preparing for colonoscopy 29
    surgery *see* colectomy; colostomy
    UC in 7–8
colonic lavage solutions 92
colonoscopy
    research 194
    to detect cancer 168–70
    to detect IBD 29, 31
colostomy
    defined 106
    for Crohn's colitis *131*
complementary therapies *102*
complications
    ankylosing spondylitis 12,
        154–55
    arthritis 59, 96–98, 154
    blood-clotting abnormalities
        164–65
    bone disease 41, 155–56
    cancer 120, 160, 165, 167–70,
        194
    eye problems 163–64
    hemorrhage 153
    iron-deficiency anemia 99,
        151–53
    kidney diseases 161–63
    liver and biliary diseases 158–61
    mouth sores 156–57
    nutritional 165
    pancreatitis 165
    perforations, abscesses, and
        fistulas 148–49
    peri-anal disease 27, 91, 93–95,
        149–51
    skin diseases 157–58
    strictures 147–48
    toxic megacolon 53, 146–47
computerized axial tomography
    (CAT) scan 33–34
conjunctivitis 163

constipation
    blood in 19
    from anal inflammation 93
    from calcium supplements 42
    from iron supplements 99
    management 92–93
    with strictures 148
continent ileostomy 110, *111*,
    112–13, *120*
contraception 16, 174
coping strategies 184–85
countries where IBD occurs 9
cramping
    after ileostomy 109
    in CD 22, 24–25, 143
    in lactose intolerance 37
    in UC 21
    on liquid diets 52
    with strictures 148
Crohn's colitis
    about 24–25
    surgical treatment 129–33
Crohn's disease
    and appendectomy 17
    and diet 44
    and smoking 15–16, 132
    complications 12, 147–50,
        152–53, 158, 161–62, 165
    diagnosing 6–7, 24, 30–34
    dietary restrictions 35
    dietary treatment 46–47, 49–50
    during pregnancy 174–75
    first identified 5
    genetic factors 11–12
    immunity factors 13
    life expectancy 179–80
    other names for 6
    prevalence 10
    recurring after surery 132–34
    surgical treatment 121–41
    symptoms and signs 7, 22–27

    what is inflamed 8
    where it occurs 8
    who gets it 10
cromolyn enemas 85–86
CT scan *see* CAT scan
cuffitis 119
cyclosporine 73, 160
cytokines 13

dairy products 39–40
deep sea diving 108
descending colon
    anatomy 4
    UC in 7
diagnosis
    in children 34, 142–43
    of CD 6–7, 24, 30–34
    of lactose intolerance *38*
    of UC 6–7, 28–30
diagnostic tools
    air-contrast barium enema 29–30
    capsule endoscopy 32
    CAT scan 33–34
    colonoscopy 29, 31, 168–70
    enteroscopy 31–32, 170
    esophagogastroduodenoscopy 32
    leukocyte scan 34
    MRI 34
    sigmoidoscopy 28
    single-contrast barium enema 31
    small-bowel enema 31
    small-bowel series 30
    ultrasound 33–34
    upper GI series 33
    X-rays 29–31, 33
diarrhea
    after surgery 125, 129
    bloody 19, 25
    caused by foods 22
    causing anal inflammation 94
    causing anal itching 95

causing mineral deficiencies 101
from iron supplements 99
in CD 22, 24–25, 45, 143
in lactose intolerance 37
in toxic megacolon 148
in UC 19
traveler's 22
with strictures 148
diclofenac 96
diet, *see also* food; nutrition
after ileostomy 109, 113
after small-bowel transplantation
146   135
calcium 40–42
children 145
clear fluids 45–46, 121
during pregnancy 176
enteral 52–54, 101, 122, 144,
176
fats 45
fiber (roughage) 4, 42–44, 55,
109
for short-bowel syndrome 134
full fluids 46–47
high-fiber 22
high-glutamine 54
lactose intolerance 36–42
liquid diet products and therapy
47–52
low-fat 45
meat 44
parenteral 52–54, 101, 135, 176
to prevent kidney stones 161
unnecessary restrictions 35,
54–56
unproven role in IBD 16–18
dietary restrictions
in CD 35
unnecessary 35, 54–56
dietitians 35, 41
digestion 1, 3, 16–17

dilatation 119, 122, 151
diphenoxylate
as antidiarrheal 88, 91, 117
during pregnancy 177
side effects 88–89
drugs, *see also specific drugs and
the table on pages 195–96*
5-ASA 61–64, 119, 165, 169,
177–78
acid-reducing 98–99
analgesics 96
and children with IBD 143–44
and the placebo effect 101, 103
antibiotics 22, 79–84, 98, 118,
141, 149, *157*, 177–78
anticoagulants 165
antidiarrheals 88–89, 117, 129,
178, 185
bile-salt binders 90–91, 127
biologicals 74–79
bulk formers 89–90
categories 58
causing diarrhea 22
containing lactose *40, 57*
cromolyn 85–86
during pregnancy 176–78
erythropoietin 101
fish oil 84
for anal fissures 91, 93–94
for anal itching 95–96
for constipation *92–93*
for hemorrhoids 91, 93–94
heparin 85
herbal products 87, *102*
immunosuppressive 69–74, 144,
177–78
lidocaine 84–85, *157*
NSAIDs 22, *96–98*
prebiotics 83
precautions 57
probiotics 83–84, 118

research 193
short-chain fatty acids 85
steroids 41, *49*, 49, 64–69,
    93–95, 143–44, 155, 157,
    177–78
sulfasalazine 58–61, 64, 151,
    165, 174, 176–78
under study 87
duodenum
anatomy 1
CD in 8, 25, 128
surgery in 128

elderly people *see* older people
electrolyte solutions 29
elemental diets 47–49
employers 190
endoscopy 32
enemas
    after surgery for Crohn's colitis
        132
    barium 29–31
    budesonide 118
    cromolyn 85–86
    lidocaine 84–85
    risks 57
    short-chain fatty acid 85
    small bowel 31
    steroidal 69
    tapwater 92
energy (calories) 39, *41*
energy loss
    in CD 22
    in UC 21
enteral diet 52–54, 101, 122, 144,
    176
enteritis
    after radiation treatment 22
    mimicking IBD 6
enteropathic arthropathy 154
enteroscopy 31–32, 170

enterostomal therapists 109
episcleritis 163
erythema nodosum 157
erythropoietin 101
esophagitis 98
esophagogastroduodenoscopy 32
esophagus
    anatomy and function 1
    CD in 8, 26, 129
    surgery in 129
etanercept 78
etoricoxib 97
Europe 9
exclusion bypass 168
exercise
    and ileostomy 108
    pain after 22
    to prevent blood-clotting
        abnormalities 164–65
extracorporeal photochemotherapy
    87
eye problems 163–64

false urge 19–20, 25
family and friends
    anger toward 183
    financial issues 186
    of adult with IBD 186–88
    of child with IBD 145,
        187–88
    unreliable advice from 55
famotidine 99
fat (in food) 45, 55, 127
fatty liver 158
feces *see* stool
female sex hormones *see* steroids
ferrous gluconate 99
ferrous sulfate 99
fertility
    after surgery 119, 173–74
    with CD 173–74

fever
  in CD 143
  in toxic megacolon 146
  in UC 21
fiber
  and IBD flare-ups 43–44
  and ileostomy 109
  excreted 4, 55
  laxative effect 42–43
  restricting 43–44
financial issues 51, 53, 185–86,
  191–92
fish oil 84
fistulas
  appendiceal 26
  defined 149
  diagrams *138*
  dietary therapy for 47
  how they form 135
  ileal 125
  ileo-vesical *138*
  mucous, of the rectum 107, *108*
  peri-anal 27, *138*, 150
  recto-vaginal *138*
  treatment 149
fistulous tract *138*, *140*
FK506 73
flare-ups
  during pregnancy 175
  of CD 26
  of UC 21
  reducing 59
fluid diets, *see also* liquid diet
    therapy
  clear 45–46, 121
  full 46–47
folate 151
folic acid 44
food, *see also* diet; nutrition
  bread 40
  broken down in GI tract 3

  causing diarrhea 22
  dairy products 39–40
  gravy *40*
  greasy or spicy 35, 55
  high in iron *100*
  "junk foods" 145
  meat *40*
  seen in stool 54–55
  with "friendly" bacteria 83
food additives 18
food poisoning 22
free radicals 17
friends *see* family and friends
fructose 22, 42–43
fruit 42–44

gallbladder cancer 160
gallstones 160–61
gas, *see also* bloating
  accumulated in colon 146–47
  during sleep 117
  with lactose intolerance 37, 39
  with strictures 148
  with UC 20–21
gastrointestinal system
  anatomy 1, 2, 3–4
  normal functioning 1, 3–5
gastrojejunostomy 128–29
genetic factors
  in cancer 167, 194
  in IBD 11–12
  research 193–94
gentamicin 80
giardiasis 22
GI tract 1, 2, 3–5
glucocorticoid steroids *see* steroids
glucose 37
glutamine 54
grains *40*, 42–44
granulocyte-monocyte colony-
  stimulating factor 79

granulomatous colitis 6
granulomatous enteritis 6
granulomatous ileitis 6
gravy *40*
growth hormone injections 79
gum infections 157

H-2 blockers 98–99
heartburn 98–99
hemorrhage 153
hemorrhoids 91, 93–95, 149
heparin 85
hepatic flexure 3
herbal products 87, *102*
high-glutamine products 54
histamine-2-receptor antagonists
    98–99
homeopathy *102*
home parenteral nutrition (HPN) 53
honey 83
hospital stays 184–85
HPN (home parenteral nutrition) 53
hydrocortisone 69, 93, 119
hydronephrosis 162
hyperbaric oxygen 87

IBD *see* inflammatory bowel disease
ibuprofen 96
idiopathic proctocolitis 6
idiopathic ulcerative colitis 6
ileitis 6
ileo-anal anastomosis
    about 113–14
    for indeterminate colitis 120–21
    how it's done 114, *115*, 116–17
    problems 117–20
ileocecal valve
    anatomy 3
    surgical removal 125
ileostomy
    1930s and 1940s 106–7

1950s (Brooke procedure)
    107–9
1960s (Kock procedure) 110–13
    and recurring CD 133
    defined 106
    loop *115*, 116
    problems 108–9, 112
    revision 112
ileum
    anatomy 3
    cancer 168
    CD in 8, 25, 123, 125–28
    surgery *see* ileostomy; resection
immune response abnormalities
    12–14
immunoglobulin infusions 87
immunosuppressive (immuno-
    modulator) drugs
    during breastfeeding 178
    during pregnancy 177
    for IBD 69–74
    in children 144
    side effects 71
incontinence
    after pelvic-pouch surgery
        117–18
    elderly people 113
independence 183
indeterminate colitis 6, 120–21
indomethacin 96
infections
    after surgery 109, 119
    role in IBD 14–15
infectious colitis 14–15
inflammatory bowel disease
    and lactose intolerance 36,
        37–42
    and life expectancy 178–80
    complications 12, 27, 41, 53, 59,
        91, 93–99, 120, 146–65,
        167–70, 194

defined 5
diagnosing 6–7, 22, 24,
    28–34
dietary treatment 35–56
drug treatment 41, 57–107
employment 190
financial issues 51, 53, 185–86,
    191–92
future 193–94
in children 16, 34, 51, 134,
    142–45, 187–88
number of cases 10
quality of life 180–88
risk factors 10–18
sexual and reproductive issues
    171–78
surgical treatment 105–41
symptoms and signs 7, 19–27
travel tips 188–90
types of diseases 5–7
who gets it 9–10
infliximab
effect of smoking on 15–16
for CD 153
for IBD 74–76, 153
for skin diseases 158
side effects 76–77
injectable steroids 69
insurance
and dietary therapy 51, 53
studies and strategies 191–92
intestinal tuberculosis 15, 22
intestine *see* colon; small bowel
iritis 163–67
iron 44, 99–101
iron-deficiency anemia 99, 151–53
irritable bowel syndrome *14*, 22,
    23–24
ischemic disease of the intestine 22
ISIS-2302 79
ISS-ODNs 87

Japan 9
jejunum
anatomy 3
CD in 8, 128
surgery in 128
Jews 9, 38
Johne's disease 15
joint pain 59, 96–98, 154

ketoprofen 96
kidney diseases 161–63
kidney stones 161–62
kilocalories *41*
Kock ileostomy 110, *111*, 112–13,
    120

lactase 36–37, 39
lactose
about 36–37
in drugs 57
in foods 22, *40*
lactose intolerance
and maintaining calcium intake
    39–42
defined 37
diagnosing *38*
diagram *36*
who gets it 37–39
lansoprazole 97, 99
laparoscopic surgery 134, *135*, 193
large bowel *see* colon
laxatives 92
LDP-02 79
leak, postoperative 119
left-handedness 12
leukocyte (white blood cell) scan 34
lidocaine 84–85, 157
life expectancy 178–80
liquid diet therapy, *see also* fluid
    diets
advantages 51

and regular food 52
disadvantages 51–52
duration 52
elemental 47–48
how it works 50
in children 144
modular products 48
polymeric 48
tube feeding 50–51
who uses it 50
why used 48–49
liver diseases 45, 158–59
liver transplantation 160
loop ileostomy *115*, 116
loperamide
    as antidiarrheal 89, 91, 117
    during pregnancy 177
lymphocytes 13

macrophages 13
magnesium citrate 29
magnetic resonance imaging (MRI)
    34
male sex hormones *see* steroids
malnourishment 151, 165
maltitol *22*, 43
maltol *22*, 43
mannitol *22*, 43
MAP kinase inhibition 87
massage *102*
MCT (medium-chain triglyceride)
    45, 48
meals
    associated with bloating 148
    pain after 22–23, 25
meat *40*, 44
medium-chain triglyceride (MCT)
    45, 48
men
    effects of sulfasalazine 61
    fertility with IBD 173–74

frequency of IBD 10
    sex after surgery 118,
        172–73
menstruation 174
6-mercaptopurine
    during pregnancy 177
    for IBD 72
    in children 144
    side effects 72, 165
mesentery 8
methotrexate 72–73, 177
methylprednisolone 69
metronidazole
    and alcohol *81*
    during breastfeeding 178
    during pregnancy 177
    for CD 80–81
    for pouchitis 118
    side effects 81–82
microscopic colitis 22
mineral oil *92–93*
minerals 44, 99–101
modular diet products 48
mouth
    anatomy 1
    CD in 8
    sores 156–57
MRI (magnetic resonance imaging)
    34
mucosa, inflamed 8
mucous fistula of the rectum 107,
    108
multiple sclerosis 12
mycophenolate mofetil 74

naproxen 96
natalizumab 78–79
naturopathy *102*
nausea
    in CD 25
    in toxic megacolon 148

on liquid diets 52
with strictures 148
nitric oxide 17
nitroglycerine 94
nizatidine 99
nonspecific ulcerative colitis 6
nonsteroidal anti-inflammatory drugs
(NSAIDs)
for arthritic pain 96–97
side effects 22, 97–98
North America 9
NSAIDs *see* nonsteroidal anti-
inflammatory drugs
nutrition, *see also* diet; food
for children with IBD 144
importance 35
nutritionists 35

obstructions
caused by strictures 147
defined 121–22
surgical treatment 122–23
ointments
for anal inflammation 93–94
for anal itching 95–96
older people
and diet 47, 56
and illness acceptance 183
and surgical treatment 113–14
omega-3 fatty acids 84
omeprazole 97, 99
onions 83
opium 88–89
oral contraceptives 16, 174
osteonecrosis 155
osteoporosis 41, 155–56
ostomies
defined 106
in children 145
side effects 129
oxidants 17

oxygen, hyperbaric 87
oyster shells 42

pain
abdominal *see* abdominal pain
chest 26
joints 59, 96–98, 154
painkillers 96
pancreatitis 165
pantoprazole 97, 99
paregoric 88
parenteral nutrition 52–54, 101,
135, 176
partial parenteral nutrition (PPN) 53
PEG (polyethylene glycol) solution
92
pelvic pouch procedure
about 113–14
for CD 133
for indeterminate colitis 120–21
how it's done 114, *115*,
116–17
problems 113–20
perforations 147–49
peri-anal disease 27, 91, 93–95,
149–51
perineum 105
peritoneum 1
peritonitis 147
petroleum jelly 95
phlegmon 139
piles 91, 93–95, 149
piroxicam 96
placebos 101–2
polyethylene glycol (PEG) solution
92
polymeric diets 48–49
potassium 44
pouchitis
defined 112
management 84, 118

PPN (partial parenteral nutrition)
   53
prebiotics 83
prednisolone *65*
prednisone
   tablet 69
   to treat CD 49, 122
   to treat IBD 41, 65
pregnancy 174–78
primary sclerosing cholangitis
   158–60
probiotics 83–84, 118
proctectomy
   and recurring CD 133
   defined 105
   for Crohn's colitis *131*
proctitis 7, 19, 62, 167
proctocolectomy
   defined 105
   for Crohn's colitis *130*
protein 39
proton pump inhibitors 99
psoriasis 12
psychological issues
   anger 183–84
   children 145
   ileostomy 108
   losses 182–83
   social 108, 145, 186–87
psyllium 90
pyoderma gangrenosum 157–58

quality of life
   anger 183–84
   coping strategies 184–85
   family issues 187–88
   financial issues 51, 53, 185–86,
      191–92
   index 180, *181*
   losses 182–83
   social issues 108, 145, 186–87

rabeprazole 97, 99
race
   and IBD 9–10
   and lactose intolerance 38
radiation treatment 22
ranitidine 99
recombinant erythropoietin 101
rectal foams 69
rectum
   anatomy 4
   surgery 105, 107, *108, 131,* 133
   UC in 7, 20
recurring CD after surgery 132–34
reflux esophagitis 98
regional enteritis 6
regional ileitis 6
relaxation techniques *102*
research 193–94
resection
   defined 105, 122–23
   diagrams *126*
   for CD of the ileum 123, 125–28
   for Crohn's colitis *131*
   for jejunal CD 128
   side effects 125, 127–28, 134
revision of ileostomy valve 112
right-handedness 12
risk factors
   blood-vessel abnormalities 16
   chemical factors 17–18
   genetic factors 11–12
   immunity factors 12–14
   infection 14–15
   nutritional factors 17
   oral contraceptives 16, 174
   smoking 15–16, 86–87, 132
   stress *14*
rofecoxib 97

sacroiliitis *see* ankylosing spondylitis
Scandinavia 9

scarring after surgery 141

Schilling test 127–28, 153

sclerosing cholangitis 158–60

serosa 8

severe colitis 53

sex factors

    IBD 10

    osteoporosis 156

    skin diseases 157

sexual activity

    after surgery 118, 172–73

    with IBD 171

short-bowel syndrome 134

short-chain fatty acid enemas 85

sigmoid colon

    anatomy 4

    UC in 7

sigmoidoscopy 28

single-contrast barium enema 31

sitz baths 94–95, 137, 141

skin diseases 157–58

skin tags 150

small bowel

    anatomy and normal function 1, 3

    cancer 166, 168, 170

    CD in 22–23, 132–33

    diagnostic series 30

    enema 31

    transplantation 134–35, 193–94

smoking 15–16, 86–87, 132

social issues 186–87

sodium phosphate solution 29, 92

sorbitol 22, 42–43

splenic flexure 3

steroids

    and breastfeeding 178

    defined 49

    during pregnancy 177

    for anal inflammation 93–94

    for anal itching 95

    for IBD 41, 49, 64–69

    for mouth sores 157

    in children 143–44

    side effects 144, 155

stoma 106

stomach

    acid 99

    anatomy and function 1

    CD in 8, 25, 128–29

    surgery in 128–29

stools

    after ileostomy 109, 112

    after surgery for Crohn's colitis 129, 131–32

    blood in 19, 25, 112, 143, 152–53

    dark-colored 99

    formation and composition 4–5

    frequent 52

    incontinence after surgery 117–18

    narrow 151

    testing 28

stress 14

strictureplasty

    defined 122–23

    diagrams 124

    for duodenal CD 128

    research 193

strictures

    of anal canal 150–51

    of bowel 147–48

sugars 22

sulfasalazine

    for IBD 58–59, 64

    safe during breastfeeding 178

    safe during pregnancy 176–77

    side effects 59–61, 151, 165, 174

sulindac 96

support

    enterostomal therapists 109

    for children 145

from healthcare team 145, 184
organizations 192
suppositories
for anal inflammation 93
for constipation 92
for cuffitis 119
surgery, *see also specific types*
and adhesions 141
and age 113–14
choice of procedures 113–14,
120
definitions 105–6
for abscesses 135–41
for CD 121–41
for hemorrhage 153
for UC 106–21, 134
in children 134, 144
research 193–94
sweats 21
swelling, abdominal 26–27
symptoms and signs
defined 19
of CD 7, 22–27
of UC 19–21

tacrolimus 73
tai chi *102*
taste fatigue on liquid diets 51
teenagers
psychological issues 145
relationship with parents 187
tenesmus 20
terminal ileitis 6
tetracycline *157*
thalidomide 74
tincture of opium 88–89
T-lymphocyte apheresis 87
tobramycin 80
toilet trips *see* bowel movements
total parenteral nutrition (TPN)
52–54, 101, 135, 176

toxic colitis 147
toxic megacolon 53, 146–47
TPN *see* total parenteral nutrition
transplantation
liver 160
small bowel 134–35,
193–94
transverse colon
anatomy 3
UC in 7
travel 188–90
traveler's diarrhea 22
treatment
alternative *102*
dietary 35–56
drugs for associated problems
91–101
drugs for IBD 57–91
surgical 105–41
unorthodox 103–4
vitamin and mineral supplements
99–101
tube feeding 50–51, 144

UC *see* ulcerative colitis
ulcerative colitis
and appendectomy 17
and smoking 16
complications 147–48, 150,
152–53, 162, 165
diagnosing 6–7, 28–30
dietary treatment 48–49
during pregnancy 174–75
first identified 5
genetic factors 11–12
life expectancy 179
nutritional factors 17
other names for 6
prevalence 10
surgical treatment 106–21, 134
symptoms and signs 19–21

what is inflamed 8
where it occurs 7–8
ulcerative proctitis 7, 19, 62
ultrasound
    as diagnostic tool 33–34
    for hydronephrosis 162
United Kingdom 9
unorthodox therapies 103–4
upper GI series 33
urge
    after pelvic-pouch surgery 117
    false 19–20, 25
ursodeoxycholic acid 160, 169

valdecoxib 97
vegetables 42–44
vitamin A 44
vitamin B$_{12}$
    absorbed by ileum 3
    decreased absorption after
        surgery 127–28, 151, 153
vitamin C 44
vitamin D 39, 41–42, 156
vitamin supplements 41–42, 101,
    127
vomiting
    in CD 25
    in toxic megacolon 148
    with strictures 148
VSL-3 83–84, 118

weight loss
    importance of preventing 55
    in CD 22–23, 25, 35, 143
    in UC 21
    regaining weight 45, 55
wheat bran 90
white blood cell (leukocyte) scan 34
women
    breastfeeding 178
    fertility after surgery 119, 173

fertility with IBD 119, 173
frequency of IBD 10
menstruation 174
oral contraceptives 16, 174
osteoporosis 156
pregnancy 174–78
sex after surgery 118–19, 172–73
skin diseases 157
work 190

X-rays 29–31, 33
xylitol 22, 43

yersiniosis 22
yogurt 40
young people 145, 183

zinc oxide 95
zinc supplements 101